PRAISE FOR MARY

"An Example for All Canadians"
To MR AND MRS STEINHAUSER: **[...]** or her outstanding courage and fortitude **[...]** ng vocation. Your daughter has set **an example for all Canadians** ... ny thoughts are with you at this trying time.

—PIERRE ELLIOTT TRUDEAU, Former Prime Minister of Canada
in a telegram June 11, 1975

"Guts and Compassion" and Modern Misjustice in Canadian prisons
Yet there are very few (prison staff) who have both the guts and the compassion to do anything about it. **Mary Steinhauser** had both these traits. She tried to help the inmates.

—CHRISTIAN BRUYERE, Playwright,
WALLS (1978) and film producer, WALLS (1984).

"A beacon-of-light inside the prison"
Mary was a beacon-of-light inside the prison. She genuinely believed most inmates could move on to healthier lives. She was "a leader in developing programs with this intention" and "the prisoners 'me to appreciate her compassion, insights, advice on survival skills and hope for the future".

—MAE BURROWS, friend and colleague at Matsqui, 2013 YWCA Woman of Distinction
Award for Environmental Sustainability, 2010 SFU Outstanding Alumni Award

"The New Testament answers that the finest Life ended on the cross. Such was the life of Mary Steinhauser, who served life faithfully and gave so much to our service."
But what is Life for? Do the good, the brave, the courageous have the best time? The New Testament answers that the finest Life ended on the cross. Such was the life of Mary Steinhauser, who served life faithfully and gave so much to our service.

—REV. J. A. NICKELS, Chaplain-General of the Canadian Penitentiary Service, in his
homily at Mary's funeral, Blessed Sacrament Church, Vancouver BC, June 16, 1975.

"The Mary Steinhauser Killing"
The single most profound incident in the 102-year old history of the British Columbia Penitentiary.... Words could hardly do justice to the memory of **Mary Steinhauser**, classification officer at the B.C. Pen.

—NEIL D. MACLEAN, Author of *Serving Life 25: One Guard's Story*

"There will never be another person who has helped so many inmates"
Mary helped many inmates when others had given up on them as hopeless cases. Why she helped us, we all knew—she just loved helping people in extreme need. How she helped them when others failed, we'll never know. Perhaps it was the way she had about her—her true concern for others. I know this because I was one of such difficult inmates… It will be a long time for many, many inmates before they forget the help that Mary was able to give them.

—MATSQUI INMATE. Name Withheld. Letter to the Editor,
Vancouver Sun June 14, 1975

Mary Steinhauser, ca.1971

BETWEEN BLADE & BULLET

the **MARY STEINHAUSER** *story*

The courageous life and tragic death of a brave and passionate young social worker and prison justice advocate, caught up in the terror of a hostage-taking at the B.C. Penitentiary in June 1975.

MARGARET FRANZ

Suite 300 - 990 Fort St
Victoria, BC, V8V 3K2
Canada

www.friesenpress.com

Copyright © 2021 by Margaret Franz
Front Cover Photo - old BC Penitentiary Gatehouse, New Westminster BC, Canada
Photographer: Erica Franz
First Edition — 2021

All rights reserved.

No part of this publication may be reproduced in any form, or by any means, electronic or mechanical, including photocopying, recording, or any information browsing, storage, or retrieval system, without permission in writing from FriesenPress.

Grateful acknowledgment is made to Peter Lynde, sketch artist, for use of his sketch.

ISBN
978-1-5255-8824-2 (Hardcover)
978-1-5255-8823-5 (Paperback)
978-1-5255-8825-9 (eBook)

1. Biography & Autobiography, Women

Distributed to the trade by The Ingram Book Company

CONTENTS

PRAISE FOR MARY i
AUTHOR'S NOTE i
   1: INTRODUCTION 1
   2: ROOTS 5
   3: GROWING UP 13
   4: RESCUED 23
   5: PSYCHIATRIC NURSE, ESSONDALE, B.C. 27
   6: 999 QUEEN STREET, TORONTO 41
   7: TRANQUILLE SCHOOL, KAMLOOPS, B.C. 57
   8: MATSQUI INSTITUTION, MATSQUI, B.C. 65
   9: EDUCATED 69
  10: THE PEN 79
  11: 41 HOURS 89
  12: REQUIEM 101
  13: 1975 FARRIS COMMISSION OF INQUIRY 129
  14: 1976 CORONER'S INQUEST 147
  15: INMATE HOSTAGE-TAKER 159
  16: GO-BETWEEN 169

17: HOSTAGE	173
18: MARKSMAN	187
19: VERDICT	207
20: SONG OF MARY	211
BIBLIOGRAPHY	**243**
ACKNOWLEDGEMENTS	**249**
ABOUT THE AUTHOR	**251**

In memory of Mary

who was robbed of her voice. It was not theirs to take.

With this book, I give it back to her,

wrapped in love.

To my beloved family, past, present, and future.
And in particular,
to the two women
who were the finest role models a young woman could ever hope
for
my mother, Johanna,
and my sister, Mary.

AUTHOR'S NOTE

Forty-five years have passed since I first began to write this story about my sister, Mary Steinhauser.

Often emotionally taxing, it has been both rewarding and agonizing to reach into my soul and give voice to the strongest, most powerful and principled woman I have ever known.

Mary had a rare combination of deep compassion, fierce loyalty and protectiveness for the disadvantaged and underprivileged, and a driving, unrelenting commitment to make lives better for the voiceless and forsaken.

In this time of the COVID-19 pandemic and the acknowledgement by the WHO (World Health Organization) of the sacrifices of nurses in designating 2020 as the Year of the Nurse, Mary stands as a proud and heroic example of her first profession, nursing, and will be remembered as an outstanding Woman in History for her final act of selfless bravery.

To do justice to her story, I relied upon my own memories; researched institutional histories and events; interviewed close friends, colleagues, clients, and admirers of Mary; solicited submissions from people who knew of or about Mary at different phases of her life; and made considerable use of my large personal collection of newspaper and magazine articles for the period of June 9, 1975 to August 30, 1976, when Mary's name was most frequently in the news.

For the latter half of this book, I have used as source documents the *Report of the Commission of Inquiry into Events at B.C. Penitentiary June 9 to 11, 1975* and the incredibly rich, detailed, minute-by-minute account of witness testimonies in the *Proceedings of the 1976 Inquest into the Death of Maria Elizabeth Steinhauser*, all 2,237 pages, which I used to support and confirm my own recollection of events as they unfolded.

Some, but not all, of the names in my book have been changed to preserve anonymity, and to add an additional layer of confidentiality, details of a personal nature have occasionally been altered as well.

I would like to thank the several participants of the events portrayed in this book for taking the time to share their memories of the events described in this book with me and, through me, with the reader. It is recognized that people can honestly remember situations, events, and conversations differently even when asked to recount what happened immediately, let alone years later. With respect to myself, I have written about my recollection of events and related them to the best of my knowledge and ability.

Reconstruction of events by artist Pete Lynde shows tactical squad charging to free hostages at B.C. Pen
This sketch accompanied the article "Probe told of Mary's last seconds" by James Spears and Alex Young, *Province* newspaper, Vancouver, B.C., June 28, 1975.
Credit: Peter Lynde, sketch artist.

```
TLX OTTAWA ONTARIO JUNE 11 940P

MR AND MRS STEINHAUSER
5887 MAIN STREET
VANCOUVER, B.C.
BT

I AM DEEPLY SHOCKED BY WHAT HAS HAPPENED AND SEND YOU MY
HEARTFELT SYMPATHY AT THE TERRIBLE LOSS YOU HAVE SUFFERED.
MARY WILL BE REMEMBERED WITH RESPECT AND GRATITUDE BOTH
FOR HER OUTSTANDING COURAGE AND FORTITUDE IN RECENT DAYS
AND FOR HER SERVICE IN A MOST DIFFICULT AND DEMANDING
VOCATION. YOUR DAUGHTER HAS SET AN EXAMPLE FOR ALL
CANADIANS AND I WANT YOU TO KNOW THAT MY THOUGHTS ARE WITH
YOU AT THIS TRYING TIME.
        PIERRE ELLIOTT TRUDEAU
        PRIME MINISTER OF CANADA


TELTEX VCR

PMO PCO OTT
```

Telegram of condolence and praise for Mary's outstanding courage to our mother and father from Pierre E. Trudeau, Prime Minister of Canada, Ottawa, June 11, 1975.

1
INTRODUCTION

Mary was three years older and my only sister, a prison classification officer at the B.C. Penitentiary. On Monday morning, June 9, 1975, she was taken hostage, along with fifteen other prison employees. Their captors were three desperate inmates intent on escaping their fortress-like prison, high on the hill overlooking the swift-flowing Fraser River in New Westminster, B.C.

Forty-one hours later, at 1:30 a.m. on June 11, Mary was pronounced dead on arrival at the Royal Columbian Hospital in New Westminster. Beyond belief, she'd been shot twice: once through the shoulder and once fatally through the heart. That bullet was fired from a gun held by a member of the prison tactical squad, who were sent into the classification area to rescue her and the other fourteen hostages.

Who knows what thoughts passed through her tired mind in those last moments before the fatal bullet penetrated her compassionate heart, when she came to understand that her colleagues had forsaken her and that the man with whom she felt she had reached an understanding was prepared to bury his dagger into her unprotected throat. How lonely she must have been when she died.

The Farris Commission of Inquiry, charged with inquiring into the B.C. Penitentiary hostage-taking and shooting, failed to supply answers for how and *why* Mary died.

Almost a year later, I came to Vancouver to attend the B.C. Coroner's inquest into Mary's shooting death, cherishing a vague hope that some truths would finally be aired publicly for all to see and for all to judge.

For over a month, the inquest had been in session. But it was at precisely 4:30 p.m. on Wednesday, June 30, 1976, when I lost any illusions I might have had about the inquest into my sister's death.

For a month, we sat on hard, straight-backed wooden chairs in the tiny coroner's court behind the Royal Columbian Hospital, listening to scores of witnesses give their version of what had transpired in the early morning hours of June 11.

For a month, we gave our attention to police witnesses, to expert witnesses, to penitentiary staff, to inmates, and to the members of the tactical squad. In their testimonies, we tried to find the common element of truth, which seemed to become, day by day, more elusive, more intangible.

For a month, we waited for the single most important witness of all, Albert Hollinger, a member of the tactical squad who, allegedly, had deliberately mixed up the guns used in the final shootout in order to conceal the identity of the man who fired the fatal shot.

And on Wednesday at 2:30 p.m. on June 30, Hollinger began his story. A slightly built, wiry man, Hollinger said that he was an expert marksman, that he had won the silver shield for marksmanship in the early '50s, that he was also a gunsmith. He was confident, he said, that he had seen no lanyard ring on the butt of his gun—a lanyard ring that adorned the gun from which the fatal bullet had issued.

Crouching low over the coroner's desk, he demonstrated graphically the manner in which he took aim and fired. First at prisoner and hostage-taker Dwight Lucas, then once in the direction of Andrew Bruce's right side, and then again in the direction of Andrew's face. "His face exploded in blood," he said as he recounted the effects of his marksmanship.

When asked if he could have possessed the bull-barreled gun with the lanyard ring on the butt – the gun that, if testimony was to be believed, materialized out of nowhere, was held by no one, and phantom-like, shot and killed Mary—he said that if he had fired that particular weapon, he would have sustained multiple bruises on the palm of his supporting hand. When Hollinger was asked if he had any concern that one of his bullets may have hit Mary, he replied in complete confidence that he had no concern whatsoever.

And yet he had been without sleep for forty-one hours. He had seen, he testified, a woman in a colourful dress standing immediately in front of Dwight Lucas just as he aimed at the top of Lucas's head. The woman, it was discovered later, was an apparition, a figment of his imagination.

Apparently, he hadn't felt any desire to assist the two injured, possibly dead people lying in a pool of blood on the floor. His main concern, he said, was to get the hostages out of the vault and to collect the guns from the other members of the tactical squad. "It was an exciting time," he said. His story was over.

It was 4:25 p.m., and the cross-examination was about to begin. In my limited experience in the coroner's court, I had found that the most illuminating, crucial portion of the witness testimony was revealed in cross-examination, when the *why* of actions was brought to light. I eagerly awaited my turn to ask questions, but some movement from the direction of the jury caught my eye.

They were seated in front of me: seven men who had been selected by the coroner to deliberate upon the reasons for my sister's death. They had grown restless. They moved about in their seats, shifting position repeatedly, and I saw the foreman glance several times at his watch as if he were anxious to be relieved of his duty for the day.

Hollinger was the last witness before the inquest was to adjourn for five days. There was a lull in the proceedings; one of the lawyers was leafing through his papers, attempting to locate a piece of information about which he wished to examine Hollinger.

And then I saw it. Reaching into his left-hand pocket, a florid-faced elderly juryman produced a roll of Life Savers. He tore off the outer wrappings, looked around, and with an apologetic half smile, reached out to offer Hollinger a Life Saver.

It was at that moment, at 4:30 p.m. on Wednesday, June 30, that I lost any illusions I might have had about the inquest into my sister's death.

Mary, my courageous, passionate, determined sister…you deserved better than that.

2
ROOTS

THERE WERE TWO SUPERSTARS IN our lives. Johanna, our mother, and August, our father. From them, we acquired strength, courage, self-discipline, and self-confidence. We learned to face issues square on, to accept reality, and to be honest and straightforward in our dealings with others.

They gave us both, Mary and me, the best years of their lives, and they were fine parents. Kind, generous, and loving. How Johanna and August came to be such good parents, I'll never know, because neither had been fortunate enough to have a nurturing childhood. They were both orphaned at a young age: August as a toddler of eighteen months and Johanna as a seven-year-old.

It was the summer of 1901, in the town of Ravensburg in southwestern Germany, when our father, the youngest of five children, was born to Francesca and Paul Steinhauser. Eighteen months later, catastrophe struck when Francesca, aged thirty-five, died quite suddenly. Her sudden death left her husband, Paul, a distraught and overwhelmed father with five children to support. For a time, Paul struggled to simultaneously care for his children while working at a brewery, but eventually it all became too much for him so he threw up his hands in despair and turned his children over to a welfare agency to farm out to foster homes in the surrounding countryside. August had just learned to walk.

August and his four siblings were never to live together as a family again. The five children were fostered out separately, becoming effectively indentured servants to their respective foster parents, who were mostly farming families in need of labour to work their land or act as domestics.

During his growing years, our father was moved from home to home, never quite sure how long he'd be staying with one family before being uprooted yet again. These were lonely years for a young boy, who for as long as he could remember was always on the outside looking in—the child who wasn't really wanted except for the value of his labour.

In spite of his fractured childhood, over the next two decades August grew into a strong and handsome young man. In 1919, at 18, he began a three-year training and apprenticeship program in a creamery or cheese-making operation, in the small village of Gornhofen, about 7 ½ miles from Ravensburg. Gornhofen was the home of many small farmers who planted small fields and bred cows, selling their excess milk to Ströbele's creamery where August worked (and probably lived). At that time, tradespeople needed to train as an apprentice. They were also required to attend a trade school, where they learned general skills such as math, accounting, and so on. After three years, there was a qualification exam, which determined whether candidates were able to complete the apprenticeship program or stay on for another year. August successfully passed this test in 1923 at the Tradesmen's Association (Handwerkskammer) in Ulm.

By 1924, Germany was in the depths of the Great Depression. Hyperinflation and high unemployment were frightening and pernicious realities. An American dollar was worth a billion deutschmarks; a billion deutschmarks bought a pound of butter, and a half-billion bought a package of cigarettes. The German people were loading their deutschmarks into wheelbarrows and taking them to the bank in hopes of getting at least a pittance for their savings, now almost worthless. Such was the case for August and his savings from several years of work.

He refused to be beaten.

Having no prospects for employment in his own country, he turned his back on his homeland and set out on the adventure of a lifetime. Borrowing $132 from his former employers for a one-way fare to Canada, he set sail on the SS *Cleveland* from Hamburg to Halifax with a final destination of Salvador County, Saskatchewan. Once in Saskatchewan, he worked as a farmhand for six months before moving to Halfway Lake, Alberta.

Eventually, he saved enough money to purchase his own farm and acreage just outside Edmonton.

For the next twelve years, August worked his prairie farm. It was an extremely difficult time. The Depression had arrived in Canada and prevented him from even contemplating the idea of marriage and a family. Things came to a head in February 1940 when a disastrous prairie fire ravaged his homestead, rendering the soil infertile for crops. At almost forty years old, our father was forced to abandon his farm, bid farewell to the Prairies, and once again start a new life. This time, he would reinvent himself as a forestry worker on Vancouver Island in B.C.

Not long after, on a trip to nearby Vancouver, August met thirty-four-year-old Johanna Henrietta Reisner. Without a doubt, "Hannah" as she was sometimes called, was the best thing that could have happened to our father. She brought him stability, love, and generosity of heart and spirit. In her arms, the streak of misfortunes which had dogged him throughout his life, finally ended.

Born in 1907, Johanna had her roots in the fascinating and opulent city of Vienna, the former capital of the Austro-Hungarian Empire. She was the namesake and only child of Johanna, a single mother, who was gentle and caring—until she inexplicably left her daughter, now seven years old, to be cared for by her own sister while she left for some distant part of Europe, never to return. The aunt and uncle, a childless middle-class couple, did their best to look after their now-orphaned niece. Though they were competent parents, neither was particularly warm nor loving and at times, leaned towards harsh discipline.

For years, the young Johanna wept for the mother who never returned.

Years later in the spring of 1938, Hitler's planes could be heard in the skies over Vienna. Our mother, now 31, was employed as a live-in governess and cook/housekeeper for a well-off Austrian Jewish family, Mr and Ms L., and their two young daughters. As factory owners in this bustling capital city, the family made a comfortable living. It wasn't long however before gruesome stories began to circulate about how Viennese Jews were being treated by Hitler's occupying SS troops who were slowly but relentlessly setting in motion their reign of terror. Business owners were forced to self-identify by placing the Star of David on their places of business and then, very shortly their properties were confiscated.

In November of that year, the infamous pogrom called *Kristallnacht* (or Night of Broken Glass) signalled the beginning of the horror that awaited the Jewish people in Nazi Germany and parts of Austria. It was a night when Jewish homes were ransacked, as were shops, towns and villages as SA Storm troopers destroyed buildings and smashed shop windows with sledgehammers, littering the sidewalks with shards of broken glass. In Vienna alone 95 synagogues were set on fire and completely destroyed.

Fearing the same fate as his countrymen, Mr L. made plans to leave Austria with his family and travel to London, England. But first he would go by himself to find suitable accommodation while his wife, our mother and the two children would stay behind in Vienna to pack their belongings.

The night finally came when our mother, Ms L., and her two daughters were ready to leave Austria. It was midnight when they boarded the train in Vienna. German soldiers and guards were everywhere at the station. After they boarded, heavily armed soldiers soon entered and asked to see their passports. They were all very quiet, hoping the train would start out without further delay. After some hours, they arrived at the German border when once again, armed soldiers came onboard and demanded to see their passports. After some tense moments, the soldiers left abruptly and the frightened passengers heaved a collective sigh of relief. After a long journey, the family arrived safely in London, reunited with Mr. L. and settled into their temporary residence in their new island home.

It was the spring of 1939 and everyone knew that war was imminent. Mr. L. decided that he wanted his wife, daughters and our mother to leave for Canada immediately, far away from the theatres of war on the continent. He himself would take a later ship in a few months. So on April 23, 1939, our mother, Mrs. L and the two little girls embarked on the *SS Montclare,* docking in Montreal just five days later. They were safe at last. Mr. L. would join them soon… or so they thought.

On September 3rd, 1939, England declared war on Germany. That same day, Mr. L. boarded the *SS Athenia* at Southhampton, eager to finally reunite with his family in Canada. Unbeknownst to him, German U-boats were silently prowling the North Atlantic seas just off the English coast waiting to strike unsuspecting passenger liners or merchant vessels sailing out of England. Only 12 hours after WW II was declared, the *SS Athenia* was the very first ship in the British fleet to be torpedoed and sunk without warning by the Nazi submarine U-30. She carried 1,417 passengers and crew bound for Montreal. In all, 93 passengers and 19 crew members died that fateful night. What a cruel twist of fate it was that one of the 93 doomed passengers was none other than Mr. L., the man who'd tried so desperately to ensure his family's safety but sacrificed his life in doing so.

As they tried to cope with their new reality, our mother must have been a great source of strength to the grief-stricken Ms L. and her two daughters when the family finally settled in Vancouver BC making it their permanent home. Throughout the next year, our mother continued to be a loving companion and governess but at the same time, she was anxious to begin a life of her own with a husband and children to love and care for. So when a handsome German bachelor named August, also expressing an eagerness to marry and have children, was introduced to her, it seemed a perfect match!

After a short courtship, Johanna and August were married in October 1941, settling down in a rented house in Lake Cowichan, B.C., where August continued to work in the forestry industry.

On August 25, 1942, their first child, Maria Elizabeth, was born at the King's Daughter's Hospital in Duncan, B.C.

Enchanted with their beautiful baby girl, they lavished Mary as she came to be known, with all their love and undivided attention. And for the next three years, Mary, a charming, talkative, pretty little girl with wavy chestnut hair and hazel eyes, was the sole object of their affections.

Everything ticked along quite nicely, and in July 1945 when I was born, our family was complete.

Two years later our father purchased, sight unseen, a $1,800 ($22,118 in 2021) property in the small village of Burton in the Arrow Lakes region of the West Kootenays in southcentral B.C. Arriving in Burton ahead of our mother, our father took possession of the 10-acre property and began to do some much needed work on the main house which was, at the time, little more than a large one-room log cabin. Among other preparatory work, a chimney had to be built and general clean-up work completed. All the rustic buildings on the ten-acre farm including the main house, barn, chicken house, root house, and granary, were of log construction and bore shake roofs. But the crown jewel of the farm was the lush orchard at the front of the property, with forty healthy fruit trees. It was magnificent! And didn't Hannah say how much she liked cherries? It all looked just fine, at least to our dad.

But not to our mother. Her first impression of our new home was a miserable disappointment. We arrived late in the evening, exhausted after a long train journey from Vancouver to Revelstoke, and then down the lake on the sternwheeler the SS *Minto* to Nakusp. The final leg was by car, a long twenty-four miles over gravel road to Burton. Our mother had never seen the property; when our father had returned home to Lake Cowichan after buying it, she naturally quizzed him about the house. His reply was, "Well, it needs a bit of fixing up."

It was an understatement, to say the least. According to our mother, the one-room house was constructed of squared-off logs with a plank floor, an attic, and a lean-to at the back. There was no running water, no indoor plumbing, no electricity, and very little furniture. Our "bathroom" was an outhouse, a short walk from the house.

A bit of fixing up, indeed! Hannah thought as she ran off into the bushes beside the house for a good cry. But the next morning, she woke up, and when she saw the beautiful mountains around her, her mood improved considerably, and she settled in to begin a truly pioneer life.

Having spent most of her life in large urban centers in Europe and Canada, Johanna regarded life on a farm in a remote area of B.C., far from any centers of culture or refinement, as a major challenge. As a young woman considering a suitable marriage partner, she once vowed that she would never marry a farmer! But here she was, a reluctant farmer's wife.

Her initiation into this new life came with some considerable adjustments. Our mother had to learn to milk a cow, no easy job! But milking cows was just the beginning—in the spring she helped with planting the garden; in the summer, she canned and preserved the vegetables and fruit; and in the early autumn, she helped August with the haying, with splitting and stacking wood for the stove and heater and the harvesting of fruit from the orchard. These tasks our mother did in combination with all her own household chores, and with very few household conveniences.

That first summer brought a bountiful harvest of fruits of all descriptions—too much, in fact, for us to use. A few boxes of prunes and cherries were shipped to Nelson, but a large portion of the harvest was left to rot. The next few years passed, but the winter of 1950/51 was a bitterly cold one—the deer were so hungry they came down from the high valleys to the barnyard to eat the hay put out for the cows. Almost ninety percent of the once lush orchard was destroyed by the cold temperatures that year.

Although she complained from time to time about how difficult it was to sustain an even oven temperature for baking on our wood-fired kitchen stove, our mother rose to the many demands of a pioneer existence, providing us all with a loving, well managed, and peaceful domestic life.

3

GROWING UP

Our farm lay about a mile and a quarter from the village of Burton, located midway between Nakusp at the north end of the Arrow Lakes and Fauquier to the south. At that time, the population of Burton was a scant two hundred souls—though some local wags opined this was an inflated figure and, in fact, the head count included cats and dogs.

Burton had had its heyday in the late 1800s, when it was generally believed that the gold to be found in the surrounding hills was the purest on record in Canadian history. It was even given the designation of "city," and town lots at the time were advertised in the local newspapers for $100 and $150.[1] But its short-lived blush of fame as a gold rush town had long since evaporated before we arrived in 1947. By that time, the majority of families in the area depended almost entirely on the forest industry to provide a living wage for the heads of households.

If a man could not or would not make his living as a logger, he had little choice but to turn to the land and cultivate, hoping to wrestle from the soil a slightly better-than-subsistence form of living. Fortunately, our father was strong and healthy and able to handle the demanding work of a lumberman, but he also enjoyed almost every aspect of farming, including animal husbandry and the cultivation of crops. In these, he was an efficient, well-organized farmer, who took great pride in possessing healthy,

---

1   Pat Philcox, ed., *Whistle Stops Along the Columbia River Narrows: A History of Burton and Surrounding Area,* Burton New Horizons Book Committee (Canada: Friesen Printers, 1982), 40.

well-groomed animals and crops that were plentiful and free of pests and disease.

Our life was the life of a pioneer family. Our home was a simple whitewashed log cabin partitioned into four small rooms. Until Mary was eleven, we had no electricity and used coal oil lamps for lighting when darkness fell. A wood stove in the kitchen and a wood-burning heater in the living room provided for all our heating needs. Every morning, we leapt out of bed, scampered across the cold linoleum floor, and stood shivering beside the heater as we quickly dressed for school.

There wasn't any indoor plumbing so water had to be drawn from a twenty-five-foot outdoor well, carried to and from the house in pails two at a time and heated on the stove for washing, cooking, and cleaning. Our outhouse stood some yards from the house and boasted two holes and plenty of graffiti from previous owners. Frequently, we pondered the significance of "Kilroy was here" carved into the side wall adjacent to some initials and hearts and arrows. Oddly enough, it was never made clear to me just who "Kilroy" was.

Although the quantity of our livestock varied from year to year depending on the success of spring breeding, we usually had around four to five cows and two or three heifers and steers. When the birth of a calf was imminent, our father was always present to help the cow deliver her calf safely. Sometimes he would be up all night "on call". When the calf finally arrived, our father would proudly announce the birth and call us up to the barn to greet the newborn.

We also had several pigs, some chickens, and a team of horses. Our favourite pets were the house cats. We detested the times when Father would announce that this steer or that pig was about to be butchered. Although we understood the necessity for butchering, we didn't like the idea at all.

There are some theories among early childhood educators that children will learn, almost by osmosis, how human sexuality behaves by using the animal world as examples. This was not so, as far as Mary and I were concerned! Although we lived on a farm for most of our developing years, it never occurred to us that what animals did by way of procreation was in any way related to what human beings did. We knew that Dad would take the cow to the neighbour's bull when she started to act weird and frisky in the springtime, and that the bull would mount the cow and thereafter we would wait to see if "it" had taken, whatever it was. Generally, in a few months, a calf would appear. We witnessed plenty of animal births and marvelled at them, but we never once made the conceptual leap between the behaviour of animals and the behaviour of people. What animals did and what human beings did were two entirely different things.

Although I never once heard Dad complain about having too much to do, there must have been times when he would have given a great deal to have two sons who could have given him more help with the endless chores on the farm. Because Mary was the oldest and the strongest, she was most often required to do the heavier, more unpleasant chores. It was she who had to help Dad with the milking, and somehow as the years went on, I avoided the requisite training for this all-important barnyard skill.

Every year in spring, Dad would say, "Well, after we've weaned Suzie's (or Blackie's or Spotty's) calf, we'll teach Margaret how to milk." But invariably, something would come up to prevent my training. Since I didn't really want to learn to milk cows anyway, I didn't press the issue. But Mary, who was very eager for me to learn so I could help her, would peevishly ask, "Dad, when is Margaret going to learn to milk the cows?"

He might agree that yes, it was time, but for some reason it never happened.

In late summer, when haying time arrived, Dad hitched up our team of horses to a wooden hayrack and we set out to our back five acres, where the neatly bunched haystacks lay dotted around the open field. From then on, Dad and Mary remained in the field to pitch the forkfuls of hay onto the waiting hayrack. Usually I remained on the deck of the rack. My job, a less strenuous one, was to distribute the loose bunches of hay around the rack so the load would be evenly balanced. Then I would stamp the hay down so the greatest possible amount of hay could be taken at one time. Haying was a hot, dusty, and tiring job that neither of us liked very well, but since we weren't a mechanized farm, it was a job that had to be done.

Our reward came when Dad declared, "Well, I guess that's it for the day."

We'd gratefully flop down at the back of the rack, high up on the sweet-smelling, prickly hay, and on the way home we'd contemplate the vastness of the wide blue sky, all the while making secret private promises to ourselves that we'd never marry a farmer.

Another job we both heartily disliked was the nightly summertime task of bringing the cows home for milking. At that time in the country, it was still acceptable farming practice to let cattle out onto public property to wander and graze the open countryside. Each morning in May, depending on the availability of grass and the weather conditions, Dad would open the gates after the milking was done and release the cows. They would wander the countryside freely until five o'clock, when it was time to bring them home for the evening milking.

After supper, one of us would take the family bike and Sandy, the neighbour's dog, and begin the hunt for our small herd of cattle. They often wandered down various dirt roads to open meadowlands and pastures. The problem was, we never knew for certain which direction the cows had taken, and there were two or three possible places they would be grazing. So it was a matter of searching, sometimes for hours if the cows had wandered beyond their usual grazing grounds. Sandy, as an eager but untrained herd dog, wasn't much help. Instead of barking at their heels to drive them forward, he barked in their faces driving them backwards which required yet another prolonged chase. Finally, we'd get them pointed in the right direction, heading home.

Since we cultivated and harvested a large vegetable and berry garden, and possessed our own source of beef, chicken, and pork, the food we ate was always of the highest quality, nutritious, and delicious. Our mother was a superb cook. The main meal of the day was generally the evening meal, at which no vegetable was served without a sauce, no meat without rich brown gravy, and no poultry without a tasty stuffing. On one hand, this was undeniably a wonderful gift; on the other hand, our hearty appetites generated some unwanted weight for both of us in our early teens.

It was impossible to resist our mother's culinary feasts or her baking. We drank glasses of rich milk, devoured homemade bread at every meal, and munched on cookies, cakes, and sweet breads for snacks. Although we worked and played hard, the energy we expended never quite seemed to match the daily caloric intake of all that delicious food. Both of us were chubby.

Kids can be cruel. Because of her extra weight, Mary was often the object of vicious teasing and bullying. The boys at school took perverse pleasure in tormenting Mary because they always got a rise out of her. Instead of ignoring their heckling, Mary shouted and screamed at them in a frenzy, threatening to beat them up or make them pay for their insults. Their response was to laugh at her and renew their ugly taunts. This only made her angrier.

I think these miserable encounters convinced Mary that she needed to be physically strong, so she decided to become a "lady" boxer. While other girls her age poured through forbidden romance magazines, Mary eagerly scrutinized every boxing magazine she could find for just one picture of a woman boxer. She found plenty of photos of women wrestlers, but woman boxers? Not to be found. Nevertheless, she engaged me in daily sparring sessions, which invariably resulted in a bruising for me. The boxing sessions took a curious turn, though, that gave me a marvellous opportunity to repay her for all the poundings I was subjected to.

One day she decided that, since dieting didn't seem to bring any miraculous weight loss, she would solicit my help in ridding her buttocks and upper thighs of excess fat. Where she got the idea, I'll never know, but she theorized that if I punched her enough in this general area, the fat would simply melt away. With her back to me, she'd stand with her hands on the wall to support herself and incite me to thump her on her buttocks.

I gladly agreed, but after punching her for a while, my arms tired. Nevertheless, she commanded, "Come on! Punch harder! Can't you punch any harder?"

After a few of these punching-bag sessions, my initial enthusiasm for what had promised to be a thoroughly pleasant task began to wane.

As she grew into her teens, Mary started to slim down and grow tall, reaching her adult height of five foot seven by the time she was thirteen. She was very pretty, with lovely wavy chestnut hair, hazel eyes, beautiful straight white teeth, and a delightful smile. As she matured, she attracted the attention of many young men. Not just men, though...everyone liked

Mary. Her easy charm and sociability endeared her to all and she could strike up a conversation with anyone regardless of gender, age, or status.

The school we attended from grades one through eight was a two-room building close to the centre of town. Grades one to four were assigned to one room, and grades five to eight to the other. Surprisingly, given the size of our small town and the lack of amenities it offered to prospective school board employees, we had some very good teachers. They each had their idiosyncrasies: one preferred teaching core subjects, the other loved piano-playing and singing, and another would stage dramas and involve students in poster-making contests. Considering the isolation and the limited resources they had at their disposal, our teachers were conscientious and hard-working.

When she began school at six, Mary was absolutely thrilled with the whole business of learning. Armed with knowledge far beyond the capacity of my three-year-old mind, she'd arrive home from school and immediately begin to teach me what she'd learned that day. Setting up a mock classroom in the attic, there she was, the teacher in front, and I, her student, in my desk waiting for her instruction. She was a no-nonsense teacher, a veritable martinet. Having little patience, she scolded me severely if I didn't pay attention to her instructions or failed to read a word properly or perform some mathematical operation. Sometimes my tears of frustration brought my mother running.

But it was unquestionably Mary's early tutelage that made my own years in school pass so smoothly. Her sound training in the fundamentals of reading and arithmetic gave me a head start in my early grades, so I sailed through my elementary school years. Mary enjoyed school as much as I did. It was, after all, the one place where we met and played with kids our own age. We walked the mile and a half to and from school every day, winter and summer, but we didn't mind. Even illness wasn't a good enough reason to miss school, and we'd protest loudly if Mother announced, "You can't go to school today, dear; you're too sick."

Mary did very well in school, but she worked hard for her marks. Perhaps it was some initial difficulty in school that gave her the doggedness and persistence that became an integral part of her character. More than anyone I knew, she worked hard to accomplish a task because she wanted so very much to succeed.

As far back as I can remember, Mary showed a genuine concern and empathy for the marginalized in society. She seemed to take the plight of Indigenous peoples and the Black community in America as a personal affront and was fearless in her condemnation of the treatment these communities received at the hands of the white man. When she was only thirteen, her teacher threatened to evict her from the classroom if she continued to make such vociferous attacks on the Canadian government for its current and former practices regarding the First Nations peoples. But banishment from the classroom and a loss of her audience was the last thing Mary wanted so from that time on, she tempered her criticism. Nonetheless, undeterred, she held forth in eloquent oratory in private conversation.

This fearless stance to bravely give voice to her convictions, in spite of the inherent risk of being muzzled by those in authority, continued into her working life as a professional nurse and social worker. It was almost as if she felt a personal identification with individuals or groups disadvantaged or in bondage, physical, mental, emotional, societal, or otherwise.

A field of suppressed energy surrounded Mary; even when she was sleeping, an aura of dynamism was an almost tangible entity that flowed from her and touched the observer. It was this restrained but palpable energy, her honesty, and a complete lack of artifice that sometimes brought her into conflict with her environment. At the same time, these were her most admirable character traits.

Mary's belief in justice and fairness were due in part to our religious upbringing. Times have changed in the Catholic Church, and rules and practices have been softened to accommodate more liberal, flexible views. But when we were growing up, challenges to traditional religious doctrine or practice weren't tolerated. Our parents were devoutly Catholic and raised us in a strict but non-oppressive environment. For its small population, Burton boasted no less than four congregations: the Roman Catholic, Anglican, United, and Pentecostal churches clustered in the centre of the village.

Twice a month on Sundays, the priest for our parish, who lived in Nakusp, travelled twenty-four miles down the lake to Burton to say mass for our small congregation. Mary and I didn't particularly enjoy the walk into town, a mile and a quarter over gravel roads, especially when we were all dressed in our Sunday finery and wearing our best shoes but we did look forward to meeting with our friends. Occasionally in the summer, visiting nuns from other parts of the province would come to our community and have summer day camps to teach catechism classes. Going to confession was a requirement as a kind of purification of the soul to be able to take communion. This bi-monthly self-inquisition forced us to be brutally honest with ourselves.

To my knowledge, Mary never lied or deliberately told an untruth. She may have been unwilling to reveal something, but when she was pressed by our mother for the truth of the matter, she would always admit to wrongdoing. Our mother always said that we couldn't hold anything from her, and Mary swore she could never look into our mother's eyes and not tell the truth.

But where Mary and I differed was in the willing acknowledgement of misdemeanours. Mary had a well-developed conscience. But on occasion, she was almost too honest and too demanding of herself, and her guilty feelings over some transgression would gnaw at her until she couldn't suppress them any longer. The relief of being able to unburden herself to Mother was worth the punishment she may have to pay for the revelation. I, on the other hand, thanked my lucky stars if I weren't found out and would, if need be, take my "dark" secrets to the grave rather than reveal them.

Like some siblings, Mary and I fought quite frequently. Strong willed and single minded, we often argued about those daily chores not prescribed and allotted by our mother. Who would do the dishes? Who would bring the cows home? Who would fill up the water pails at the well? At these times, I considered Mary to be bossy and unreasonable, while she considered me a wimp and lackadaisical. We used various methods to manipulate each other, the most popular being a form of blackmail.

It was exquisite agony for the victim and a delicious sense of absolute power for the blackmailer. If one of us was lucky enough to find the other in a compromising situation or to unearth some secret that we knew would bring down our mother's wrath on the hapless one, we milked the situation for all it was worth and for as long as we could. We extracted promises of "I'll do anything you say, just don't tell Mom," and thereupon outlined our demands. A verbal commitment not to reveal some transgression in exchange for favors could last for a week, a month, or if it were something really "good" that we had on the other, even six months, until the threat of telling no longer brought the transgressor to her knees in fear and trembling.

Sad was the day for the blackmailer who felt her power evaporate when the victim threw off her fear and said, "Go ahead. I don't care. You can tell Mom."

Probably the times when one of us was being blackmailed were the quietest and most peaceful in our household because there would be no arguments about who would do this or that. The blackmailer, armed with her dreadful knowledge, had only to glance meaningfully at the other and the victim would capitulate with barely a murmur. It was cruel but effective.

I remember vividly the time Mary held her dreadful knowledge over me for at least six months. I was in my early teens, and a Western movie starring my current crush, Scott Brady, was playing that Saturday night in the community hall. So as not to miss a second of the action, my friend and I were seated close to the front of the hall. Every time Brady strode or rode onto the screen, we gushed and tittered so obsessively and loudly that, after a couple of unheeded warnings, the hall manager decided she'd had enough and told us to leave the theatre. Unfortunately for me, Mary was also at the theatre, seated across the aisle with her own friends, and observed every second of my excruciating walk of shame out the front door.

It seemed a lifetime before I worked up the courage to defiantly challenge Mary and end my season of torment and servitude.

Although Mary was not naïve, she was always frank, open, and candid in her dealings with others. Because she herself was straightforward and aboveboard, she expected others to be the same and was sometimes hurt when a friend would reveal themselves to be underhanded, secretive, or deceptive in some way.

On certain occasions, Mary lacked diplomacy and artfulness, which brought her into conflict with others. She scorned sophistry and ostentation and could be quite cutting in her private condemnation of those who cherished ideas of self-importance. Never mean-spirited, some of her attitudes were echoes of our parents' beliefs about displays of wealth, the acquisition of "things," and the outward show of status and consumerism. A strong and principled attitude of quiet pride in the value of hard work, a dedication to family, and a duty to live a good life were the unspoken but lived experience of our parents.

Mary had a big heart. She was extremely sensitive to the suffering of the disenfranchised or disadvantaged. Whenever she could, she would attempt to alleviate pain, whether mental or physical.

She was fifteen years old the day that Amy almost drowned.

4
RESCUED

It was hot and humid that summer day in August 1957 when my friend Amy and I set out for our favorite swimming place—the flooded meadowlands abutting the Lower Arrow Lakes. Amy was eleven and I was twelve. We asked Mary if she'd like to come with us, but she was busy and said she might come later on.

We walked down the gravel road, past several neighboring farms and through the forest, until it opened up to reveal the vast expanse of standing floodwater. The swift-flowing Columbia River was just visible beyond the natural levee that separated the river from the flooded grasslands. We were lucky; the typically ever-present swarms of mosquitoes that often plagued us around stagnant water were lethargic that afternoon. Save for their half-hearted, indifferent buzzings and whinings, the atmosphere was hushed; barely a ripple disturbed the still waters, green and murky from the tangled masses of marsh grasses floating just beneath the surface.

We began to wade leisurely in the waist-deep water, a few yards from and parallel to the shore.

We'd been trying to teach ourselves to swim that year, so we were trying to stay in the shallow waters.

Since there was no such thing as swimming classes in Burton, learning how to swim was a slow, painstaking process for both of us. Through some considerable effort, I'd mastered the rudiments of the dog paddle, but Amy was still unable to even stay afloat.

Although Amy was younger than me, she was about three inches taller. We continued to wade out further, side by side in the murky water, until it was shoulder deep. Suddenly there was a curious sort of gasp from Amy and a frightened sputter. "Margaret!"

I turned to look at her, but she'd disappeared beneath the water. It crossed my mind that she was playing a trick on me, but before I could complain, the ground gave way beneath my feet.

Initially, we were both too surprised to panic. We each struggled to find solid footing, but very soon it was apparent that our thrashing about had driven us further away from shallow ground. By a series of convulsive twistings and turnings, Amy worked her way closer to me, then reached out and grabbed me by the shoulder. Her hand was a vise pressing me down into that green slimy water. A death grip.

"Let me go!" I screamed. Amy was no longer my friend; she was my most desperate enemy. We'd done so many things together, but now I was fighting for my life. If she hung on to me, she'd surely pull me down and we'd both drown.

I fought against her.

"Help me!" she cried.

"Let me go!" I sputtered, prying at her fingers.

We gasped and choked, water filling our mouths and noses. I saw the terror in her eyes. We bobbed up and down, straining desperately for air. With one mighty push, I cast her off.

I was free!

Terror gave me strength. I paddled quickly to the shore and dragged myself up through the shallow water, dropping down into the warm brown muck on the bank. I lay there sobbing and shaking. After a few moments, I pulled myself upright and peered across the water. Amy was bobbing up and down, but each time she sank, it took longer for her to surface again. I began to shout, "Amy, over here!"

Paralyzed, I watched her struggle. Then she went down for the last time, and the ripples in the water died away. The afternoon sun cast a golden, eerie glow over the now quiet face of the pond. I knew I needed to go in after her, but I had no strength left.

Why I screamed for help then, I'll never know.

The forest lay between us and the nearest home, at least half a mile away. Even if someone could hear me, they couldn't possibly get to Amy in time. Perhaps I screamed because there was nothing else left to do or because I felt the loss of my friend. Ripped from the centre of my being, my cries for help echoed and re-echoed through the forest and back to me, shattering the still of the late afternoon. They were cries of utter despair; I knew that no one would answer.

Then…a voice?

"Margaret? Margaret!"

Oh God help me, I was dreaming. Had someone really heard me?

It was Mary. "What's the matter?" she cried, still out of sight.

"Hurry! Amy's drowning!"

She burst through the trees, breathing hard. "Where is she?"

"Over there!" I cried, wildly gesticulating in the direction I'd last seen Amy's head. There was nothing there, not even a bubble to mark the place she'd gone down.

Without a moment's hesitation, Mary ripped off her clothes and dove into the water. Her strokes were strong and confident. She dove down and came up…Three times, she surfaced empty-handed. But on the fourth try, she appeared with her arm supporting Amy's head and shoulders. Cradling Amy's head in the crook of her arm, she slowly swam to shore until she was able to stand in waist-deep water. Galvanized into action, I waded out to meet her, and together we heaved Amy's limp body onto dry land.

Amy looked dead. Her face was blue, her lips dark purple, and her nostrils dilated. Strands of gummy marsh grass clung to her hair. I shuddered.

But she had a pulse. Mary set about massaging her back. "Help me!" she cried.

For about ten minutes, we took turns pushing and kneading Amy's back, in and out, up and down, stopping from time to time to see if there was any sign of life.

Nothing. Not a twitch of a muscle. Not a move in that lifeless body.

Then a shudder, a convulsive spasm. Amy moved! She coughed up green vomit.

"She's alive!" Mary gasped.

We cleared away the spittle from her mouth. Amy moaned and spit again. We lifted her upright and stroked her face and hair.

"Amy…are you okay?" Mary pleaded. "Can you hear me?"

Amy began to shake. Then, she nodded.

God in heaven, she was alive.

We held her head up, rocking her back and forth in our arms, murmuring soothing, gentle words.

After some time, Mary said, "Stay with her; I'll go get help. Maybe the Robazzas are home." With that, Mary disappeared into the forest and I could see her no more.

"Margaret," Amy whispered, "pray for me."

And so I began. Hail Mary. Holy Mary. Our Father. Whatever prayers came to mind.

For an hour we prayed together, the sound of the sacred words comforting us. Presently, we heard men's voices and the trampling of twigs and cracking of branches. It was Mary, returning with a group of men. The men scooped Amy up in their arms and carried her out through the forest and back to her home.

Fortunately, Amy recovered quickly from her ordeal and suffered no long-term ill effects.

There was some talk among the townspeople that Mary really ought to get a medal for her actions, but nothing came of it. Burton was a small town, and heroic deeds, no matter how impressive, rarely made the big town newspapers. As a matter of fact, it wasn't even reported in the *Arrow Lakes News*.

In spite of the lack of public recognition for her bravery, Mary's actions on that day served as a harbinger of the courageous woman she would one day become.

It was the day I recognized how truly brave and selfless my sister was.

5
PSYCHIATRIC NURSE, ESSONDALE, B.C.

No institution other than the B.C. Penitentiary had such a powerful and lasting influence over Mary as Essondale (now Riverview) Mental Hospital,[2] that sprawling complex of buildings some twenty miles (32 kms) east of Vancouver. The facility treated, housed, fed, and sometimes buried the majority of those who were classed as mentally ill or mentally challenged in southwestern B.C. in 1960.

It was here that Mary came into contact with all the faces of mental illness—from the severely deformed, bedridden perpetual "child" to the severely psychotic. Every possible iteration of what was considered mentally ill in the sixties was present at Essondale. For the next three years, the hospital was her training academy, domicile, and workplace. In those years, Mary's naturally compassionate and tolerant nature evolved to become foundational elements of her character.

For many of the Burton townsfolk, the name Essondale conjured up mostly negative images of a sort of jail, full to the brim with frenzied, demented madmen and women who bit and clawed and fought to free themselves from their prison. Their keepers, it was believed, were poorly paid, sadistic turnkeys who flogged and beat them their patients regularly. But the truth was quite different.

---

2   Wikipedia, *Riverview Hospital (Coquitlam),* https://en.wikipedia.org/wiki/Riverview_Hospital_(Coquitlam).

What was Essondale? Named after Dr. Henry Esson, the provincial secretary of B.C. in 1909, Essondale was the term used to describe the structures that occupied one thousand acres of government land at the junction of the Coquitlam and Fraser rivers. A person didn't ever have to leave Essondale, because it was like a small city: completely self-sufficient. It had kitchens, a laundry, a bakery, a mortuary, laboratories, a fire department, an RCMP detachment, a post office, tennis courts, a bowling alley, a barber shop, a beauty salon, a library, a swimming pool, and a graveyard. It even had a large farm where fresh fruits, vegetables, and meats were grown and harvested, to be used in the hospital's daily menus.

But Essondale was a hospital, a hospital for the mentally ill. Its essential components were the various structures that housed the patients who arrived there from all parts of British Columbia.

The first component was Crease Clinic, built in 1948. With a patient population of 265 (April 1, 1960), it was the psychiatric unit for Essondale and the admitting centre for the entire complex. This massive brick building, with its baskets of trailing flowers suspended from the porticos, was the heart of Essondale. It stood in the foreground, and through its doors passed those for whom life had become too difficult to navigate. Some came voluntarily, brought by relatives or friends whose tear-stained faces bore the agony of the decision they were making. Some came handcuffed, silent and broken or cursing and struggling against the medical or law enforcement personnel who restrained them. For most it was a temporary stay, but for some unlucky ones, Essondale would be their home and their final resting place. Crease Clinic was where it all began.

The second largest component was the Provincial Mental Hospital, which had a patient population of 3,019 (April 1, 1960). It was made up of four buildings. The first two were the West Lawn building, opened in 1913, and the East Lawn building, opened in 1930, which were the asylums for the relatively stable chronic patients, male and female respectively. The third was the North Lawn building, opened in 1955, which was the medical centre for Essondale. In addition to beds for patients requiring medical care, it also had two wards dedicated to the treatment of tuberculosis patients. Centre Lawn, opened in 1924, was the admitting centre for patients who required more extended care than the three-month maximum period provided for at Crease Clinic, but for whom there was a good potential for eventual cure and discharge.

The third component, opened in 1946, was Valleyview, the geriatric centre for Essondale. Its patient population of 657 were the old, the crippled, and the bedridden, those whose minds and limbs were atrophied by the ravages of time. It wasn't likely that anyone who had been admitted to Valleyview would ever leave.

The fourth component was Woodlands School, a complex of buildings with some units almost a century old, situated on the north bank of the Fraser River. Woodlands was the home for those with mental disabilities, or the "mentally retarded," as they were formerly referred to. Over a thousand developmentally delayed adults were institutionalized at Woodlands, and they were classed in the most demeaning terms as "idiots," "imbeciles," or "morons" according to their mental ages and their potential for training. For many, in particular the severely challenged, there would never be any hope of leaving Woodlands.

All walks of life and classes in society—the rich, the poor, the old and the young, professionals and labourers alike—were represented at Essondale. Their states of mind were given strange and forbidding names: catatonic, hebephrenic, schizophrenic, manic-depressive, psychoneurotic, pathological, asocial and anti-social, sexual deviant, alcoholic and drug addicted. Many of the residents of Essondale had symptoms of more than one illness, and their treatment was made more difficult because they were convinced that the real problem lay, not with themselves, but with other people or events over which they had no control.

As one patient replied each time Mary asked how he was feeling, "I'll be out of here as soon as the Doc gives me my brains back."[3]

In 1960 Essondale had its own training school and on-site residences for the psychiatric nurses who were to staff its many wards. It was widely advertised throughout the province that a student nurse accepted into training would not only receive a monthly allowance but would be charged a pittance for room and board for the duration of their training and for six months thereafter. From all parts of B.C., dozens of young women and men interested in nursing as a profession, but unwilling or unable to afford

---

3   From M. Franz private correspondence.

the high cost of tuition and living expenses to become a registered nurse in a general hospital, were lured to Essondale to take advantage of this amazing offer. In the brochures that promoted the exciting and challenging opportunities of psychiatric nursing as a career, there was no mention that Essondale was no place for the weak or timid and that the training could destabilize a more sensitive, delicate nature.

In her final year of secondary school, Mary learned about psychiatric nursing from her guidance counsellor. The training allowance of $113 a month and the low-priced room and board were a magnet. It seemed almost too good to be true. Here was an opportunity to acquire a profession and get paid while doing it! She had always wanted to be a nurse, and it seemed unlikely that she would ever break into the boxing world as a lady boxer or make inroads into the world of music as a singer—two alternate ambitions she once held. She applied for admission to Essondale and was accepted to begin training in September 1960.

Our parents were totally supportive of Mary's career plan. They were both very keen that Mary (and I) would have a profession or interesting professional employment. Burton was a small village, economically stagnant, with no large industries or companies that could employ young women or men once they graduated out of secondary school. The youth left in droves for the larger, livelier, more prosperous centres elsewhere in B.C.

I don't believe that Mary, or anyone else she spoke with in Burton, had any idea what a "psychiatric" nurse was required to do. When her ambitions became known among the townspeople of Burton, there was much discussion on this point. After some time had elapsed, it was the general consensus of opinion that a psychiatric nurse was required, in the line of duty, to bodily restrain the "crazy" people at Essondale. Neighbours and friends viewed with some trepidation Mary's decision to train at Essondale and cautioned her, among other things, to look behind her at all times.

More than anything, it bothered Mary to hear people mispronounce the word "psychiatric," and I often marvelled at the air of disdain with which she corrected people, attesting to the fact that she felt much superior in her understanding of mental health issues than the less enlightened townsfolk of Burton village.

Late in August of 1960, Mary arrived at Essondale. Her room on the top floor of Nurses Home #1 was sparsely furnished. There were two four-drawer dressers with a mirror, two sagging mattresses supported by brown wooden frames, two tiny closets, a white porcelain sink with hot and cold taps, and a radiator that groaned in agony as if it were possessed by the mournful spirit of a previous inhabitant. Tiny pink throw rugs broke the monotony of the varnished fir floors, but the walls were bare of any ornament save for the occasional pinhead nail that had borne some other nurse's cherished memento. It was not an impressive room, but it would be home for Mary for the next two years.

When she entered the room for the first time, she noticed a slim, dark-haired girl sitting forlornly on the bed beside the door.

"Hi," Mary said amiably.

"Hi," the girl answered. "I'm June Layton. I guess we're going to be roommates. I hope you like rooming with me."

"I don't see why not. Where are you from?"

"Burnaby," June replied. "Where are you from?"

"Well, it's hard to explain. Do you know where Vernon is?"

"Uh-huh."

"Well, we live, my mom and dad and sister and me, about a hundred miles east of Vernon, in a small town called Burton. It's got a population of two hundred and fifty, and that's counting the cats and dogs and rats!"

When the laughter subsided, June used the silence to study Mary more closely. Mary began to unpack her suitcase, carefully removing pictures of friends, her make-up, and clothes. She was a trifle chubby and definitely a bit knock-kneed. The charcoal-and-white box suit she wore contrasted nicely with her reddish-tinted shoulder-length brown hair, but something seemed out of order. Her eyebrows were penciled in black! *What a strange combination*, June thought, but her silent musings were interrupted.

"When do we start classes?" Mary asked, looking up from her packing.

"On Monday, at 9:15 in the Education Building, wherever that is."

"Let's go see if we can find it, have a look around," Mary exclaimed, and together they hurried out, passing and greeting other arriving nurses in the hallway.

Classes began on August 20 and, in the tradition of beginning students everywhere, Mary and June were completely absorbed with the learning of so much that was new and interesting. In those first few weeks the student nurses were given instruction in medical nursing—such things as how to take a patient's temperature, determine pulse rate, take blood pressure readings, and give an enema; how to lift patients; how to give bedpans; and how to provide for the many physical needs of patients. They were given instruction in pharmacology, anatomy, physiology, psychiatry, and psychology, and through the use of films and demonstrations, the students were taught how to deal with the mental patient.

In addition, as psychiatric nurses, they were expected to interact with the patient in an emotionally caring manner. Their function on the wards was to draw the patient out, to listen, to be empathic, and to be objective in a supportive way. They were also taught not to take any abuse, verbal or physical, from the patient, but if a patient showed hostility, the nurse was told to allow the patient to do so. As one instructor remarked in a demonstration of this point, "If a patient tells you he can't stand your guts and he's going to plough you through the wall, ask him how long he's felt that way about you, and if he feels the same way about his mother or his father. Keep him talking; get him to open up."

The students were cautioned never to strike a patient, and that they were to use the minimum amount of restraint to protect the patient from himself, or to protect themselves or other patients. The primary method through which a patient was "cooled down" was through the use of tranquilizers, the wonder drugs in use since the mid-'50s, which had brought about profound and lasting changes in the treatment of the mentally ill.

Prior to the introduction and use of tranquillizers, psychiatric nurses working in mental institutions had been little more than prison guards. The only method they possessed for controlling violent patients was the use of physical restraints, such as the straitjacket, a shirt with long sleeves laced on the patient to render their arms temporarily useless, or wet or dry sheet packs, hot or cold sheets or blankets that were wrapped around patients to relieve convulsions, relax contracted muscles, and generally sedate the combative. Rarely were combative patients released into the community to resume their normal lives since their violent moods could return any time, or so it was believed.

Nurses were often placed in impossible positions of having to control hysterical patients to prevent injury or death, either to the patient or to others, without having any permanent, lasting treatment to ensure that the outburst would not reoccur or that the patient's mental state would remain stable for any length of time.

With the advent of chlorpromazine, the first and most common of the tranquillizers, the patient became accessible to the nurse. They would now listen, could be talked to and reasoned with. Although still suffering from delusions, the effects of the tranquillizer were to provide a cushion between the delusion and its impact on the patient's mental state. As one instructor remarked, "The mental patient still sees the snakes and feels their bodies entwining around his, but he no longer cares."

And that was of great significance.

After six weeks of classroom instruction, June was given her first practicum on a female ward, and Mary was assigned to a male post-operative ward, where her patients had a variety of medical problems but were hospitalized for a relatively short period of time. She was very happy about her assignment.

"June!" she cried as she rushed through the door of their room after the first day of ward duty. "You should see the sweet little old man on my ward, he's adorable—has three little tufts of hair on his head, no teeth, and the nicest smile I've ever seen. His name is Mr. D. You should just see him!"

"Really?" June replied. "Sounds like you've got a better ward than me. At least some interesting cases. The first thing I noticed on my ward was the stench of urine. Positively hits you in the face when you walk through the door. It's just terrible! It's bad enough to be there for eight hours, I wonder how the patients can stand it."

"Hmm…I guess they get used to it…"

"But Mary, you should see the beds! Every single mattress has the shape of a human body on it, and they sag to the point where I can't see how the patients can sleep at all. Their backs must be permanently damaged!"

"I didn't notice any sagging mattresses on my ward—maybe they're treated better when they're sick."

June was silent.

Mary began. "There's a young fellow by the name of Bob on my ward. He couldn't be more than twenty-two, and June, he has the most beautiful brown eyes I've ever seen. The charge nurse told me that he's had his appendix removed and could be back on the ward in a few days. Apparently he's a pyromaniac—you know that type that just can't stop lighting fires? I talked to him for a while today, and he asked if I would be there tomorrow. Hard to believe that someone who looks so innocent could be so mixed up."

"Yeah, it's strange, isn't it?"

"And June, there's another fellow who looks like Paul Newman—honestly, I swear he looks a bit like Newman. He tried to slash his wrists when he found out that his wife and child had run off with another man, so they brought him in here for treatment. I sure feel sorry for him."

And so the two girls talked through the night. June was horrified by the physical conditions she'd seen on the wards, but Mary saw only what was beautiful and deserving of compassion; she accepted the ugliness as a necessary part of the hospital setting. June was concerned with the outward appearance of things, while Mary looked beyond the obvious for the times and occasions where she could help to alleviate the pain and anguish of her patients.

Perhaps this difference in perspective was due to their differing backgrounds: June came from a middle-class suburban family, and Mary from a rural farming community. Mary wasn't accustomed to luxury, so the absence of it didn't concern her—and certainly, she was accustomed to repugnant odours. After all, hadn't she risen each morning on the farm to milk the cows? And hadn't she been met at the barn door with a malodorous bouquet of animal smells?

For the next few months, the girls were occupied with their respective duties on the wards. Mary continued to speak of her "sweet little old man" or her special "cutie pie," but for June, the conditions she observed were becoming more and more difficult to tolerate. When June was placed on the ward Mary had first been assigned to, she looked for the "sweet Mr. D" and saw a toothless, wrinkled old man, crippled and persistently incontinent.

What in God's name could Mary find to love in that horrid creature? June mused. *She must have some special insight that I don't have.*

Mary was perturbed by the physical deformities she saw and by the lack of control some patients had over their bodily functions. She was disturbed by the cataleptic patients, those who refused to move or talk and remained in a kind of stupor, their bodies rigid and immovable. She silently wept for the patients who never had a visitor on visiting days and for the "children" of Woodlands, who could never leave their beds because of their misshapen limbs and disabling deformities.

She was frightened sometimes, too, especially by Annie B., one of the most feared patients at Essondale. Annie had been locked up in a room for years and was only allowed to leave on special occasions. She was mean and hard looking, and when the nurses saw her smile, they got out of her way, for it didn't matter who it was, Annie would move right in on you like an arrow.

The student nurses were never allowed to go into her room alone because she could choke or strangle them in a minute with her incredible strength. On one occasion, a charge nurse had turned away from Annie; in a flash, Annie had crawled up on her back. It took six nurses to drag Annie to her room.

Sometimes, too, the abusive and obscene language the patients used would bother Mary, but it wasn't long before she became indifferent to it. In fact, it wasn't long before many of the things she had considered abnormal or strange in the first few months of her training became commonplace and much less troubling.

One practice, however, that Mary found extremely disturbing was the administration of electro-convulsive therapy (ECT), which they called "shock therapy" at the time. Her first exposure to ECT was shortly after she'd completed her assignment on the male post-operative ward in North Lawn. She was assigned to a psychiatric ward in East Lawn, and one morning the charge nurse requested that Mary take a female patient,

Mrs. White, downstairs to the dormitory where the shock treatments were administered.

The doors of the ward were unlocked for Mary and her patient, and they swung open to reveal two rows of beds. Approximately twenty women, apparently drugged, lay passively on the beds. At the far end of the dorm, Mary saw a portable enclosure arranged around one of the beds. There was some activity inside the enclosure, as occasionally the curtain would be punched by an elbow or an arm. It was quiet inside the enclosure, but every so often someone from inside would say, "Hold that shoulder!" or "Oxygen, quick!"

Suddenly, out of nowhere it seemed, a nurse brandishing a hypodermic appeared at Mary's side.

"Just lay your patient down, will you? She hasn't had anything to eat, has she?"

"No, I don't think so," Mary replied, and did as she was told.

Quickly and efficiently, the drug was injected into the patient's arm.

"What was that?" Mary queried.

"It's a muscle relaxant called anatine" was the reply.

"And why is it given?"

"Well, it reduces the severity of the convulsions after the electric shock. If it isn't given, the patient could suffer a fracture."

Mary waited beside the bed as the drug slowly took effect, all the while watching as the doctor, the team of nurses, and their strange-looking equipment advanced from bed to bed, each time drawing the curtain round so that it was impossible to see what was going on.

Finally, it was Mrs. White's turn.

As the curtains were pulled around, one nurse smeared a jelly on the patient's temples, another placed a rubber mouthpiece between her teeth, while another held her knees, firmly pushing them into the mattress. Two remaining nurses grasped her shoulders and her thighs and placed all their weight on them to hold her fast in one position.

Mary looked at Mrs. White. Her eyes were wide and dilated with fear.

Then suddenly, without saying a word, the doctor, who until then had been standing quietly by, produced a pair of black tongs, approximately two feet in length. For a moment, Mary thought they looked like the tongs our father had used to stoke the ashes in our wood burning heater, but then she noticed long cords that ran from the ends of the handles to a small black box on a movable trolley. On the face of the box were dials and buttons of various sizes and descriptions.

When Mrs. White spied the tongs, she moaned piteously and shrank away from the doctor. He advanced towards her and quickly placed the tips of the tongs on either side of her head where the jelly had been applied. He turned and nodded to the nurse who stood beside the black box. She pressed a small red button.

The effect of the electrical charge was instant. Violent spasms shook the patient's body. Her eyelids fluttered, her lips trembled, and every nerve and muscle twitched and shook uncontrollably. Her right leg, temporarily free from restraint, kicked wildly up and struck a nurse on the shoulder. There was a muffled curse and together the team, fighting to keep her from thrashing off the bed, tightened their grip on her shoulders and knees. Gradually the convulsions slowed and became less intense.

Momentarily they ceased, but so had the patient's breathing.

In one brisk movement, a nurse removed the mouthpiece and inserted an airway into the patient's throat. She squeezed the bulb to force oxygen into her throat and then squeezed the adjoining bulb to force oxygen into her lungs. Within moments Mrs. White began to breathe normally again. The nurse, wiping beads of perspiration from her brow, turned to Mary and said, "Whew…I'm sure glad it wasn't me."

Mrs. White slept for an hour, and in that time Mary pondered the implications of what she'd just witnessed. She wondered what possible value there was in such a drastic and crude treatment. Obviously, it was dangerous, but she'd been told in class that the effect of the shock treatment was only temporary. It tended to confuse and disorganize the thought patterns of the patients, subduing them and making them passive and pliable. But wouldn't the electrical charge damage some of the brain cells? And wouldn't repeated treatments severely impair the cognitive abilities of the patient? And what about the effect on the heart and other vital organs? Could the body withstand such a violent assault without some permanent, perhaps hidden, damage?

"Where am I? What time is it?" Mrs. White whispered, interrupting Mary's thoughts.

Mary answered, and for the next few minutes she spoke soothingly to the woman, who appeared to be suffering some amnesia.

"I'm hungry," Mrs. White said, so Mary gave her toast and coffee.

Later that evening, in the quiet of their room, Mary discussed her fears about ECT with June. They concluded that the possible dangers of the aftereffects of the treatment far outweighed any temporary alleviation of depression or suicidal tendencies. Surely there were drugs that could be used to achieve those results. Intuitively, the young nurses had come to the same conclusion that doctors and administrators reached some fifteen years later. In an interview at Essondale in the summer of 1976, the director of Crease Clinic stated that within ten years, ECT wouldn't be around.

A few days later, Mary returned to her room after her shift and found June sobbing wildly, throwing all her clothes and belongings into her suitcases.

"What are you doing?" Mary cried.

"I'm going home," June wailed. "I've quit and I'm going home!"

"But why?"

"I've had it; I can't take it anymore! I'm so depressed and upset all the time, and I'll go crazy unless I get out. Today I saw a woman whose shoes were three sizes too small for her, and do you know? No one even noticed. She couldn't even walk around, just hobbled! This woman is so broken by the system that she can't even get up the courage to ask for another pair of shoes!"

Mary listened and sympathized, for she knew there was no point in trying to convince June to stay. There was nothing she could do to inspire June to continue her training. In order to survive in the hospital setting, Mary had learned to develop some imperviousness to the more distressing aspects of her job. She'd learned to laugh and find humour in the most unlikely places, and so retained some objectivity. On the other hand, June had permitted the ugliness to affect her. Rather than leaving the job behind at the end of shift, she carried it with her until the following day. Finding no beauty or humour in anything she observed, she became so despondent that everything weighed on her. It destroyed her effectiveness as a nurse.

Tenderly, the two women kissed each other, and as June waved goodbye, she promised to keep in touch. Sadly, Mary returned to her room, and through the night she reproached herself for not having talked with June more often. *Maybe if I'd been a better friend to her, she'd still be here,* Mary thought. Then again, it was apparent that June just wasn't cut out to be a psych nurse. Not everyone was.

Mary continued in the program for the next year and a half, gaining in confidence and skill as she honed her nursing skills with patients having differing needs. She made many friends among the nurses, both male and female.

Two stood out—the first was Allan I., a tall, handsome, blue-eyed nurse with curly blond hair and an endearing old-world charm coupled with a droll, mischievous sense of humour. Skydiving was his passion. From the moment they met, they were attracted to each other. They started to date almost exclusively.

The second was Sandra K., a nurse and fellow colleague. Tall, personable, kind-hearted and fun-loving, Sandra had a penchant for travel. She soon became Mary's close friend and confidante.

It was a proud day for all of us that spring day in 1962 when Mary received her diploma in Registered Psychiatric Nursing. For the next year, she worked on various wards at Essondale while she searched for other work, preparing for her next adventure. In the spring of '63, she resigned her position at Essondale, setting out across Canada in her battered-up vintage Ford for the city of Toronto, where she had a job waiting for her at the Ontario Hospital, the largest psychiatric hospital in Ontario on 999 Queen Street.

Little did she know how different and challenging this new position would be.

6
999 QUEEN STREET, TORONTO

After driving east three thousand miles across Canada for six days, Mary and our mom, her travelling companion, finally approached the outskirts of Toronto. It was a late spring evening in '63, and the city was dark and still. The streets were empty except for the occasional scrap of discarded paper tumbling along, chased by a gust of wind from the lake.

After dropping our mom off at a motel, Mary set out to meet up with Al at the corner of Bloor and Bay streets in downtown Toronto. She pulled off the road, parked, turned on the car's dome light, and retrieved her street map from the glove compartment. After studying the layout of the city, she pointed her car in the direction of their designated meeting place.

Mary could feel her excitement mounting as she neared their meetup location. A month had passed since they'd last seen each other and Mary had sorely missed Al. Her eyes were red and bloodshot from the strain of driving nonstop for the past twelve hours, but when she spied him standing in the doorway of an office building, her fatigue evaporated. Quickly parking the car, she jumped out and ran to meet him. Tears of joy and relief were on her cheeks as he held her close.

"I missed you," she murmured, and for a very long time they stood, their arms wrapped around each other, oblivious to the curious glances of the occasional pedestrian who passed by.

Al had already begun working as a psychiatric attendant at the Ontario Hospital on 999 Queen Street in Toronto. Applying while she was still employed at Essondale, Mary had finally received word that a position as a psychiatric nurse at the Ontario Hospital would be available for her on her arrival in the city. She was to report for duty on the afternoon shift the following day.

"What's it like, Al?" Mary asked, as they sat discussing their plans for the next day.

"Well…somehow I don't think you're going to like it," he replied cautiously.

"Why, what do you mean?"

"Oh, let's not talk about it now," he said. "You'll find out soon enough. Did you really miss me?"

So Mary was left to form her own impressions about her new place of employment when she reported for duty the following afternoon.

Essondale was far from the frenetic busyness of Vancouver's city centre. Almost park-like, it occupied some of the most desirable acreage in suburban Coquitlam. The Ontario Hospital could not have been more different. It sat on the south side of Queen Street, one of the noisiest, most heavily trafficked streets in Toronto. From the early morning hours till late into the night, the streetcars clattered by, their gong warning any careless or preoccupied pedestrian of their impending approach.

In 1963, when Mary began work there, the Ontario Hospital had celebrated its one hundred and seventeenth birthday. Of grey stone and brick, its neoclassical design and advancing age had prompted health planning authorities to consider the hospital ripe for a much-needed makeover. As population exerted pressure on the existing facilities, additions were made to the main building, and these adjoining structures were connected to the original buildings by covered walkways. Perhaps if the hospital had been situated in another part of town, surrounded by maples and great expanses of well-manicured lawns, it would have been an imposing, even grand edifice but squatting as it did among the taverns and warehouses of Queen Street, it resembled a once-dignified matron cheapened by the shabbiness of her companions.

As a graduate psychiatric nurse in the hospital, Mary held a relatively important position. In the pecking order on the wards, she ranked immediately below the charge nurses, who were generally registered nurses with little or no formal training in the treatment of the mentally ill. In a discussion with her charge nurse the first afternoon on duty, she was surprised to learn that the Ontario psychiatric hospitals had no affiliated training schools as Essondale had. Apart from psychiatric nurses trained in other countries or provinces and now working at Queen Street, the entire professional staff on the wards, both male and female, were made up of registered nurses, who had at the most three months of specialized training in the treatment of the mentally ill. The nurse's aides and cleaning staff were for the most part recent immigrants to Canada, whose philosophy of treatment of the mentally ill was vastly different from what Mary had been accustomed to at Essondale.

Before she went to work the following day, Mary and Al met for lunch. He was visibly preoccupied.

"What's the matter?" she asked.

"You know, Mary, I don't think they really know how to deal with mental patients here."

"Why do you say that?"

"Yesterday," he began, "a young guy about my age was brought into admitting. He was drunk and hallucinating. Every time one of the attendants tried to get close to him, he started to somersault all over the floor. About six of them formed a ring around him and started to close in on him."

"Then what?"

Al continued thoughtfully. "You know, even to me, those guys looked menacing. If I'd been him, I don't think I'd have let them get close to me either."

He paused to light a cigarette. "Well, they weren't getting anywhere. He was bouncing all over the place and no one wanted to get near him. So I just walked up to him and put my arm around his shoulder. He was quiet then and I started to talk to him, but the other guys saw their chance and moved right in. He pushed me away and started to hop around like a frog."

Mary's eyes were wide with curiosity.

"Finally, four of them caught him and punched him around a bit before they gave him a needle. You know, back at Essondale, we'd have handled him differently. We usually grabbed a mattress and pushed a hard-to-handle patient like him into a corner. No one, not the patient or any of the staff, would get hurt. He'd be given a shot of chlorpromazine and that would be the end of it. Here it seems as if they *want* to push the patients around."

"Hmm…I don't like the sound of it," Mary replied. As they rose to leave, their faces wore the growing concern they felt.

Apartment hunting was a chore, but within a week Mary found what she wanted—a one-bedroom suite on Jameson Avenue, a street of moderately priced apartment units not far from 999 Queen Street. It was only a few days later when Sandra K., her friend and colleague from Essondale, arrived in Toronto to join Mary and Al at the Queen Street Hospital. Sandra had a specific reason for coming to Toronto, which was to move one step closer to Europe and a vacation on the continent.

The two young women managed to arrange their shifts so they worked together. As the weeks progressed, they became more and more disgruntled with their positions and the working conditions at the hospital.

There was the case of Dino, a young man who'd been hospitalized after a "nervous breakdown." Mary had been working with Dino for about a month. She used every possible occasion to talk with him about his personal problems and he was almost well enough to be discharged, feeling that he could cope with the outside pressures that had brought him to the hospital in the first place. Dino was standing in line waiting to get into the dining room when a tough, aggressive patient standing directly in front of him challenged him to a fight. A male nurse, seeing the disturbance and assuming it was Dino who'd instigated the fracas, moved in on him. There was an intense fight and Dino was sent off to his dormitory. No one had noticed he'd been hurt.

Later on that night, as she was making the rounds on the ward, Mary noticed that Dino's neck was swollen. She reported it immediately, and he was transferred to the medical ward. The following day she learned that Dino had been sent home—according to the medical reports, he'd contracted a case of mumps and the hospital wasn't equipped to treat or house isolation cases.

A few weeks later, a report was returned to the hospital from Dino's family physician. Apparently, Dino had a torn thyroid cartilage, the result of a judo blow delivered by the male nurse that night in the dining room.

"I'm just sick of this place," Mary complained to Sandra as they discussed Dino. "Can you imagine how he's feeling, knowing that even the staff in the hospital didn't care enough about him to help him? Not only that, but that the attendants would deliberately injure him? And then the irony of it all—that a doctor here would diagnose his problems as mumps!"

"You know something," Sandra interjected, "we're probably the only ones here who know anything about psychiatric nursing—"

"You're right. Here they treat people like castoffs, instead of real people with problems."

About a week later, shortly after the patients had been settled down for the night, a twenty-one-year-old man was brought to Sandra on her ward. He had come in off the street, hopelessly drunk on Catawba—a cheap wine. The bottle that dangled in his right hand was empty, but unaware of this fact, the boy occasionally lifted the container to his lips, sucking noisily for any remaining drops of liquid. White foaming spittle dribbled from the corners of his mouth. His face was flushed and sweaty.

Sandra took his arm and asked, "Have you taken any pills?"

He winked at her. "Whaddya think?"

"I think you have."

"Yeah, I took some."

He was quiet and docile when Sandra took him to the male attendants on her ward and handed him over, but he visibly stiffened as they roughly snatched at his arms.

He jerked his arm away and screamed, "Leave me alone, will ya? I didn't do anything!"

The response was swift and savage. One attendant elbowed him in the neck; the other kneed him in the hip. "Shut up, you idiot!"

He began to shout and scream, fighting wildly to get away. They gripped his arms, twisting them behind his back. He was pushed and shoved into a sideroom, where he was quickly strapped to a waiting cot.

"Start the wet pack!" an attendant ordered.

The "wet sheet pack," long considered obsolete as a method of restraint for agitated patients at Essondale, was still being used at the Ontario Hospital in 1963. In all the time they'd been in training at Essondale, and while employed as graduate nurses there, Mary and Sandra had never actually observed the wet pack in use. Although, they'd learned of its existence by their instructors as an obsolete method of physical restraint now replaced by the tranquillizer, they were aghast at the frequency of its use on combative or unmanageable patients at Ontario Hospital.

A second bed was quickly wheeled into the room where the patient lay, still screaming his bitter denunciation of the attendants who held him down so unjustly. Quickly, a rubber sheet was stretched across the waiting cot. Seven folded sheets soaked in ice water were laid crosswise over the rubber sheet, their ends overhanging the sides of the bed. In a few brisk movements, the patient was unstrapped and pulled to the waiting bed. Six attendants held him down, and one by one the sheets were draped on him, first crossing the body from right shoulder to left side, then draping over the body from the left shoulder to the right side. Each subsequent sheet restricted more closely the patient's limbs, until finally it was impossible for him to move at all. Like a modern-day mummy he lay, scarcely able to twitch a muscle.

"Why are you treating him like that?" Sandra cried. "He was okay until you started to pick on him. Why didn't you leave him alone?"

Two of the attendants looked up at Sandra and advanced towards her. In a harsh, grating tone, one attendant screamed, "Shut up, you stupid bitch! What do you know about lunatics anyway?" And he slammed the door in her face.

Sandra was left quivering and shaking in the empty corridor.

As a result of this incident, Mary and Sandra became vocal in their frustrations with the practices at Queen Street. They decried the fact that staff members would play cards with each other while on duty and rarely, if ever, played cards or games with the patients. They felt that the wards were so understaffed that it was impossible to do any real psychiatric nursing or to talk with the patients in any meaningful way. They seethed when a doctor would prescribe medication over the phone without having seen the patient and then only supplying one-eighth of the medication that was needed to sedate the patient. They detested the use of the wet sheet packs and wanted to know why they were still being used when tranquillizers could achieve the same calming effect. With these and other complaints, they approached their supervisor, an elderly nurse who'd been the charge nurse on the ward for the past ten years.

Her answer was short.

"Keep your ears and your eyes shut, girls, and mind your own business. Things have always been done this way at Queen Street, and that's the way they'll stay. So take my advice and keep quiet about things you don't like."

Mary was furious at how they were dismissed and reprimanded. Then and there, she decided she had to get out of Queen Street as soon as she could. But in the meantime, she would encounter one of the strangest and most perplexing cases of her young life.

Judy Taylor was her name. She was fifteen years old, about five foot seven, with dark brown hair and eyes. She would have been pretty except for the sallow paleness of her skin. Her hair was cut in a ducktail fashion, and when Mary first saw her in admitting, there were bandages on her wrists indicating a recent suicide attempt. The "tracks" or "ladders" on her arms denoted a heavy use of heroin. After she was given the admission bath and was comfortably dressed in a white bathrobe, Mary began to take her history.

It was during these first few minutes that Judy interrupted Mary's questioning with "I'm a butch broad, you know…sure you want to talk to me?"

With barely a moment's hesitation, Mary replied calmly, "You're my patient and I'm talking to you."

How could someone so young be addicted to drugs? Mary wondered. Lacking the harsh, weathered appearance of the older addict, Judy's soft vulnerability seemed to cry out for help. It was a silent plea that Mary could hardly ignore. She talked at length with Judy, questioning her about her family life, her education, her peer group relationships, and her hopes for the future. After the interview was over, Mary walked with Judy to the dormitory.

As she turned to leave, Judy murmured, "I like you, nurse; will you talk to me again tomorrow?"

It was a touching entreaty.

And so the tomorrows came and went, and each time they parted company, Judy would plead, "I like you, Mary. You're my only friend, you know, and I don't know what I'd do without you. You'll talk to me again, won't you?"

"It's all right Judy; I won't go away. I'll be here again tomorrow, and we'll talk again. Maybe you could look up a friend or relative. Didn't you meet anyone you liked at school or someone you could call up and talk to?"

"Oh, those idiots, they don't understand me. If they found out how I live, they wouldn't pass the time of day with me. I've been on the streets for two years," she bragged, "and those guys," she made an obscene gesture, "they're still sucking their thumbs. What do they know about life?"

She studied Mary's face for a reaction and, seeing the discomfort there, quickly added, "But then," and her face became soft and childlike, "now that you're going to help me, I know I can change for the better. I will…I know I will, but you've gotta help me. If you don't, I'll probably go back to what I was doing."

"Listen, Judy," Mary protested. "You're smart enough to know that you've got absolutely no future on the streets. For a while, you'll find ways to support your habit, but in time, you'll most likely overdose and possibly die. Don't be naïve! You're still young enough to change your life. Don't you want to have a better life?"

"Okay, I'll really try," Judy said. "But you've got to promise to help me!"

"Yes, I will," Mary said as she rose to leave.

About a month later, Judy was considered well enough by the hospital psychiatric staff to be discharged. Her demeanour had improved greatly, and her optimistic outlook contrasted sharply with the defeatism she'd displayed at her admission. Her intentions were, she said, to apply for welfare, to stay off the streets, and to try to get into some kind of technical job training program. All the signs were encouraging.

On the morning of Judy's discharge, Mary dropped by the ward to see her. Her few belongings were scattered over the bed. Her face was alight with buoyant anticipation.

"Well, I see you're ready to go," Mary said. "Just dropping by to wish you all the best of luck and to tell you that I'll be thinking of you."

Judy recoiled as if she'd been struck a terrible blow. "What do you mean?" she cried. "I thought you were going to help me find a place to live and keep me company sometimes. How the hell can I manage without a friend?"

"But you know I'm your friend," Mary consoled her.

"But what good does that do me—just to know you're my friend?" She threw out her hands beseechingly. "Why don't you act like my friend?"

Mary sighed. "Okay, Judy…tell me, what you want me to do."

Her face visibly brightened. She looked at Mary slyly, gauging her response. "Well, what are you doing tomorrow?"

"I was going to visit my mother's friend in Hamilton."

"Well, maybe I can come with you then?"

"Uh…I don't know…" Mary's voice trailed off.

Tears welled up in Judy's eyes and began to trickle down her cheeks.

"Okay, that's fine…You can come with me if you really want to."

"Oh, thank you, Mary!" And the tears were swept away by a trembling hand. "I won't get in your way."

Over the next few weeks, Judy's demands on Mary's time and attention increased to the point where Mary rarely had a moment to herself. She'd already overextended herself by taking on a part-time job at a snack bar near the George Bell Arena in order to make more money. Combined with her regular shift at the hospital, it meant that Mary was getting a maximum of three or four hours of sleep a night. Fatigue and frustration followed her with every footstep.

To add to her stress, her relationship with Al was less satisfying than it had been such a short time ago. Al, it seemed, was becoming more distant from her. He was less attentive and affectionate, almost aloof on the occasions when she did see him. She, in turn, was snappy and irritable with him.

The fun and laughter had almost entirely disappeared from their relationship when one day Sandra said, "Say, why don't you come to Europe with me? We'll quit our jobs and get away from all this. Have ourselves a ball! Forget everything here! If we work hard, pinch our pennies, we'll have enough to leave by May. That'll give us four months to save about a thousand dollars each. How about it?"

Mary thought for a moment, and then with sudden determination, she declared, "Yes, damn it all...Yes! Yes, let's go!"

But Judy would have to be told.

A few nights later, the time seemed right.

Sandra and Mary, along with their two new roommates, also nurses, invited Judy over to their apartment for dinner. The meal was superb -- chicken roasted to golden brown, baked potatoes with sour cream and chives, fresh asparagus tips, and for dessert, a creamy blueberry cheesecake.

Judy was expansive and light-hearted. For the occasion, she'd worn an attractive floral dress; her hair, set in soft curls, framed her appealingly youthful face. She looked happier than Mary had ever seen her. Perhaps, Mary mused, the pattern of one's life really can be changed for the better. Maybe, just maybe...she'll stay off the streets and get off drugs permanently.

But how can I tell her? Mary agonized as Judy and the other girls chatted about the day's events.

The hour was getting late. Judy had to be told.

"For God's sake, Mary," Sandra whispered irritably. "You've got to tell her; it's almost time for her to go. What are you waiting for?"

"Okay, okay...I'll tell her."

A lull in the conversation gave Mary an opening. "Judy, I have something to tell you...Sandra and I have decided to go to Europe in May! What do you think of that?"

Judy's face was a study in conflicting emotions. For a moment, she sat immobile, as if paralyzed. Then her countenance twisted into an ugly grimace. She jerked around to face Sandra and screamed, "It's you, isn't it? You've never liked me, and now you're going to take her away from me! I hate you!"

And with that, she leapt out of her chair, tore across the room to the hall closet, jerked her coat off the hangar, and headed for the door.

Before she slammed out of the apartment, Judy yelled to no one in particular, "You'll regret this!"

In the still of the room, where the aromas of dinner lingered heavily in the air, the girls sat in stunned silence.

Finally, Sandra laughed nervously. "I don't think she liked that idea very much!"

In the hospital, the busiest shift is the day shift, when patients are fed, washed, and given their medications and exercises. During the late afternoon and graveyard shifts, when patients have bedded down for the night, the nurses often played cards or read. Sometimes, although it was officially forbidden, they might have a quick, discreet drink with a colleague.

On this particular evening at 999 Queen Street, Mary had taken a few minutes longer on her break to talk with a young intern, who kept a bottle of rye locked away in his desk for just such friendly occasions.

"Hi, Mary!" he greeted her. "How the hell are you?" He put an arm around her shoulder and kissed her affectionately on the cheek.

"Don't, Bob," she said nervously and slipped out from under this grasp. "I want to talk to you."

"Okay," he said. "What about? I'm your friendly listening ear—talk away!"

"It's about Judy," she said. "Did you know that she's been readmitted?"

"No, I didn't," he replied thoughtfully. "When did she come in?"

"This morning about ten o'clock. She's slashed her wrists again. I'm so worried about her. She was really upset when Sandra and I told her we were going to Europe. Honestly, Bill, I feel so responsible for her."

"Hey, wait a minute. Hold on here...Why do you feel responsible for her? You're not her mother!"

"Yeah, I know. But she's so possessive of me. I don't know how to keep her at a distance without making her feel I've rejected her completely."

"Listen, Mary. Judy has to live her own life. She can't use you as a crutch forever."

"I know, I know...but she has no one else to care about her."

"Don't worry, Mary; maybe go see her tomorrow." Bob reached out to pat her arm.

But before Mary had a chance to reply, the door to the office burst open, smashing loudly against a nearby desk.

There, standing silhouetted against the dark of the corridor was Judy.

Wild-eyed and distracted, she paused momentarily, as if uncertain what to do next. Then silently, without taking her eyes off them, she advanced to where Mary and Bob were standing, Bob's hand still resting on Mary's arm.

In her hand, Judy held a three-inch switchblade knife.

Mary and Bob gaped at her, stupefied.

Before either could utter a word of caution, Judy reached out and grabbed the front of Bob's shirt. She stabbed wildly at him.

"Ow-w-w!" he cried, clutching his hand.

Blood, thick and crimson, trickled out between his fingers.

There was a brief struggle, and somehow, between the two of them, Mary and Bob managed to wrestle Judy to the ground and extract the knife from her hand. Bob held her arms behind her back while Mary gave her a tranquilizing shot. After the medication took effect, they returned her to her ward.

"Christ…" Bob breathed when Judy was settled down again and she and Bob were alone.

"Do you see what I mean? What am I supposed to do?"

Bill looked perplexed. "I guess the only thing you can do is let her cool off a bit. Try to find out why she feels so strongly about you. We'll have to report this, you know."

"I know that," Mary replied, "but she probably won't speak to me again."

"I wouldn't be so sure about that," Bill mused.

As the spring wore on, the day of their departure for Europe, June 12th, came ever closer.

For the sum of CA$252.52 each, Mary and Sandra had booked their passage with the SS *Arkadia,* departing from Montreal, crossing the Atlantic, and finally docking in Le Havre, France. For another $221 each, they purchased a Eurail Pass entitling them to travel first class on most European trains for a period of four months.

Their ambitious itinerary through Continental Europe was impressive. Belgium and Holland in June; Germany, Switzerland, and Austria in July;

Italy, Monaco, France, and Spain in August; and England and Ireland in September. Their departure date from Liverpool, England, was October 8, almost four months after their arrival in Le Havre.

As their departure date drew closer, they became more and more excited.

Finally, June 11 arrived. On that evening, sounds of music, laughter, and clinking glasses floated through the open windows of their Jameson Avenue apartment to the street below. A wild farewell party was in progress. Mary and Sandra, the guests of honour, were flushed and excited as they were repeatedly toasted.

"Hey," someone shouted, "leave a bit of Europe for us!"

"And don't break too many hearts either!"

"Bring back a count or a duke or someone rich!"

"Hey, Mary," someone shouted above the din, "your phone's ringing."

"Just a minute," a flushed Mary replied. "I'm coming."

She picked up the dangling receiver and stood for a moment listening to the voice at the other end. The colour slowly drained from her face. The conversation lasted for only a minute.

"Yes," she murmured before she hung up, "I'll be there."

Mary's hand trembled as she reached out for Sandra, who stood nearby chatting with a friend. "Sandra!" she said in a barely audible voice. "Sandra!" This time she shook her arm.

"What's the matter?" Sandra turned to face Mary.

"We've got to go. The police just called. Judy was discharged from the hospital this morning and now she's threatening to jump from a balcony apartment three stories up on King Street."

"Wha-a-at?" Sandra's tone was incredulous.

They slipped quietly away from the party and tore over to the King Street apartment building, just a few blocks away.

The glare of powerful search lights pierced the darkness and illuminated the figure of Judy, dangling perilously on a balcony ledge. The two women rushed through the open front door of the apartment block and clambered breathlessly up to the third floor, where uniformed figures were milling about.

Mary ran up to a policeman who appeared to be in command. "I'm Mary Steinhauser," she said. "Judy was asking for me."

"Oh, yes," he replied. "She wants you. Try to get closer and talk to her."

Mary did as he suggested, and for a full hour she talked with Judy, imploring her to come in from her dangerous perch.

Finally, the assembled crowd breathed a collective sigh of relief as Judy, now clinging to Mary's arm, walked back into the apartment.

"Oh, Mary! I'm so glad you came. You won't leave me now, will you?"

"But, Judy, you know I can't stay with you…We're leaving tomorrow for Europe, remember?"

Judy nodded.

"I'll write you a postcard from time to time…Goodbye, Judy," Mary whispered as a policeman gently took Judy's arm, shouldered aside a curious onlooker, and guided her into the back seat of the waiting police car.

Judy's face was waxen until she spied Sandra hovering anxiously in the background. Her screams splintered the sultry June night. "You dirty, filthy, suspicious bitch! I love Mary, and you're taking her away from me!"

The police car quickly pulled away into the King Street traffic.

The last thing Mary and Sandra saw as they turned to make their way back to the apartment was Judy's face, twisted and drawn, glaring back at them from the windows of the police car.

Late into the evening, Mary agonized over what had just happened. What could she have done? What should she have done? How did it all become such a mess?

But the urgency of their upcoming trip distracted her.

The following morning, Mary and Sandra were given a rousing send-off by their friends. As they all waited for the train to Montreal, the good-natured ribbing and laughter mingled with tears of sadness in the group as they recalled all their good times together.

For a long time, Al and Mary stood apart from the rest and talked, both knowing that their relationship was in trouble. Would it survive a four-month separation?

Mary knew she was never going to return to work at 999 Queen Street and would most likely be heading back to B.C. once she came back to Canada. As for Al, his long-term plans were ambivalent.

Making a tentative plan to keep in touch and get together once Mary returned, they kissed each other one last time, and then Mary boarded her train where Sandra was waiting, and their European odyssey was about to begin.

7
TRANQUILLE SCHOOL, KAMLOOPS, B.C.[4]

At the foot of Battle Bluff on the northeast shore of Kamloops Lake in southcentral British Columbia lies a tract of land known as Tranquille. It was named after Chief Tranquil of the Secwepemc Nation, who in the 1830s used the area as their winter camping ground. In February of 1965, Tranquille and the institution that occupied this very site was my destination.

Mary had returned from Europe in November. In her postcard from Toronto she wrote, "I'm back. Had a fabulous time! But now I'm broke, have to find work. Coming back to BC shortly. Possible job at Tranquille, Kamloops. Think about coming up to visit after Xmas. Love Mary."

Named Tranquille School, it was a provincial training facility and permanent care home for the developmentally disabled, and it was here at this very institution that Mary was now employed as a psychiatric nurse and where I was headed via CN passenger train from Vancouver. I was going up for a few days to visit her.

Tranquille School hadn't always occupied this bucolic environment in the heart of cattle country. The semi-desert central plateau area in southcentral B.C. had originally been settled by the Fortune family, who were lured to British Columbia during the Caribou Gold Rush and subsequently stayed to establish the Fortune Ranch in the Tranquille area. Because of its

---

4   Jordan Keats, "History of Tranquille," blog essay, http://blog.jordankeats.com/history-of-tranquille/.

warm, dry climate and excellent locally grown food, the Fortune Ranch soon became a destination for people with chest complaints from all over B.C. Here they boarded for a time, and most improved in health during their stay at the ranch.

In 1906, Tranquille attracted the attention of Dr. Fagen, health officer and founder of the Anti-Tuberculosis Society of British Columbia, who purchased the Fortune Ranch and operated it as a sanatorium for several years. In 1921, however, the cost of operating the sanatorium became an impossible financial burden for the original owners so it was renamed the Tranquille Provincial Tuberculosis Sanatorium and subsequently taken over by the B.C. government and placed under the provincial secretary's department.

In the ensuing years, the search for a vaccine for tuberculosis (TB) continued, and with the development of the streptomycin vaccine, the incidence of TB around the world became much less prevalent. Adding to the reduction in TB cases was an improved understanding of the role that a better standard of living, especially better nutrition and improved hygiene, had on the spread of this once deadly epidemic. As a result, by 1958 incidences of tuberculosis had so dramatically declined that the sanatorium at Tranquille was rendered obsolete.

In its place, Tranquille School, a provincial training facility and permanent care home for the developmentally disabled, was established on April 1, 1959. Reflecting the philosophy and vision of the founders, the residents of Tranquille were referred to as "trainees" or "students" who were attending a "school," not patients who were in a hospital. In July of that year, the first group of twenty-five student/trainees was welcomed to the school; by July 1965, there were 580 student/trainees, and a new building for an additional 104 student/trainees was almost complete. At the time, the Tranquille School complex resembled a small village, occupying hundreds of acres of land adjacent to Kamloops Lake and boasting at least forty buildings.

There was still snow on the ground when I arrived, and it was cold enough that I warmly dressed for the trip. I was especially proud of my brand new purchase, a fluffy white faux-fur winter hat in the style of

Russian winter headgear. I thought I looked really cool and exotic—I was 19, and looking good was important to me.

I was really eager to see Mary again. Although she wrote the occasional postcard from famous places in Europe, I was eager to hear, in person, the stories she would no doubt have to tell about her trip around the continent. Mary was a great storyteller.

The train pulled into the Kamloops station, where Mary was waiting for me. She was in great spirits and quickly whisked me off to her new quarters, Nursing Home #1, where we'd be sharing her room for the next few days.

After I unpacked, we set out on a tour of the buildings and grounds that were Mary's home and worksite for the next year and a half. As we walked, Mary was greeted with genuine warmth and obvious affection and admiration by everyone we met—the staff, her colleagues and medical professionals, and the student trainees. Everyone seemed to know her and like her immensely. As we made the rounds, she proudly introduced me to her new community, and I basked in the reflected glory of this woman, my sister, so greatly admired and liked by everyone. It was going to be a great visit.

As we walked, she talked. The size and scope of the facility was impressive—it wasn't just a couple of buildings, it was a small village. There were residences for trainees and staff, wards for the trainees, and a host of amenities like a dentist, library, cafeteria, canteen, and even greenhouses.

In the distance we could see open farmland. Officially known as the Tranquille Farm and under the jurisdiction of the B.C. Department of Agriculture, it consisted of 300 acres of irrigated farmland and 300 acres of natural meadow. Grazing on this tract of land was a purebred Holstein dairy herd of approximately 150 head, of which 85 were milking cows. In addition, there was also a herd of 500 purebred Yorkshire hogs and a commercial beef operation of 500 head.

A modern abattoir on the site handled the beef and pork products, and a large vegetable garden was cultivated on-site. Milk, cream, meat, and both summer and winter vegetables were supplied to Tranquille School, while the surplus was distributed to provincial institutions in the Kamloops area. With a view to improving beef stock for British Columbia ranchers, some research was also conducted on Tranquille's resident beef herd and the findings put to practical use for those requiring it throughout the province.

All of this was very interesting to Mary and me. After all, we were farm girls and knew a fair bit about cows and pigs and their habits! Especially pigs.

Whenever she was asked where she came from, Mary replied that she lived on a farm in the West Kootenays for most of her childhood. She loved to regale her audience with stories of our pet pig, Petunia. One spring, Petunia's mother, our neighbour's sow, produced a healthy litter of twenty piglets. Unfortunately, she only had seventeen teats for the piglets to suckle on. For those in the know regarding pig behaviour, if a piglet can't find a teat to suckle on, without human intervention, they're doomed. The strongest and biggest of the litter always manage to latch onto a teat, but the smaller, weaker ones will be pushed aside. Within days, they'll die for lack of milk. They had absolutely no chance of survival unless taken under the wing of a kind-hearted farmer's wife or child, who could be persuaded to bottle-feed the piglets every few hours. Hence it was that on that spring day, Mr. Balaam, our neighbour, arrived on our doorstep with three tiny pink pigs mewling and crying.

Their fate was in our hands.

Our mother was smitten, and so were we. We had to try to save them.

But over the next week, in spite of our mother's constant attention, two of the tiny piglets succumbed, leaving only one. We named her Petunia.

Petunia didn't really believe she was a pig. She thought she was a dog. We babied her and raised her in the house for the next six months. She was very affectionate, and every school morning would follow us girls down our long driveway to catch the school bus at the gate. She even learned approximately what time we'd be returning in the late afternoon, and when she saw the school bus pull up and disgorge us, she'd come running to greet us, oinking and squealing her delight at our homecoming.

Eventually Petunia grew too large to keep in the lean-to at the back of our house, so she moved to the pigsty near the barn, along with the other two adult pigs. Petunia became part of the folklore of our family, a story Mary repeated many times for her colleagues and friends throughout her life, including her time at Tranquille.

But there was much more to see and learn at Tranquille in the next few days.

What I learned at Tranquille School, both from Mary and from my own observations, was how visionary the founders of Tranquille were in their approach to the treatment of the mildly to severely disabled persons in their care. The choice of "school" as a descriptor for this institution revealed its focus on the ability of every resident to learn, no matter how limited their physical or mental capacity. Every resident at Tranquille was referred to as a "trainee," even if they were totally bedridden and had multiple physical and mental incapacities, some so severe they required constant nursing care. In these instances, the training program included encouraging the trainees to learn to crawl, to walk, to feed themselves, and to do whatever they could to help themselves.

Trainees were grouped on wards according to their mental age and ranged in chronological age from the teens to sixty-five years. Each of the ten wards at Tranquille housed a defined population of trainees. For example, at one of the wards in Lakeview, the population consisted of seven male and thirty-three female trainees, seven of whom were classified as babies. All of the trainees were both physically and mentally handicapped and required constant nursing care. Staff members were urged to remember that the trainees "need and respond to love and affection from the staff members."[5]

For several of the wards at Tranquille, the idea was to completely rehabilitate the mildly and moderately disabled, and train them for a future life in a boarding home in the community. The focus of the training was to help the trainee develop life skills, such as social mannerisms and deportment, and good personal hygiene. They were taught how to avoid hazards when going downtown, how to cross the street, how to handle a telephone, how to manage money, and how to select and buy appropriate clothing.

But on the ward Mary took me to see the following day, many of the trainees were far from being able to reach even the most modest of goals outlined for trainees at Tranquille. It was a sight I will never forget, and the time I realized what a uniquely gifted person Mary was. I'd never been to

---

5   From M. Franz private correspondence.

any ward in a school for the developmentally delayed, or even a ward in a psychiatric hospital, so I was completely unprepared for what I saw.

The trainees had been brought down by their caregivers to a large playroom, where they were arranged around the perimeter of the room. I say arranged, because all were unable to move of their own accord. The most mobile of the group were in wheelchairs, with some very limited capacity to move their heads or limbs, or to talk. The least mobile were placed on mats on the floor, unable to crawl or move at all. Many had faces that were contorted or misshapen in unusual ways, or limbs that were twisted and deformed. I was stunned and shaken by the sight of so many bodies and faces so sadly and painfully disfigured.

But not so for Mary.

Beginning at one side of the room, she greeted the first wheelchaired trainee in a jovial manner, smiling and reaching out to convey her pleasure at seeing him. His response was immediate—he smiled and tried to give voice to his joy at seeing Mary.

As I was taking in this vision of the power of Mary's effect, I looked around the room and saw something really miraculous. All the patients, whether they were incapable of sustained movement or had little capacity to respond, even to visualize, slowly moved their heads in the direction of Mary's voice. They tried to smile, to gurgle or mumble a response, but one thing was clear: they were happy to hear my sister's voice and wanted to feel the warmth of her affection.

She continued around the room, cheerfully teasing some, joking with others, completely at home and comfortable with all. All of her actions were genuinely warm and sincere, nothing was forced or superficial.

For years afterwards, I pondered what I observed that day. How different I was from Mary! How was it that Mary could so easily see something beautiful to know and love in all those sweet but sadly disfigured bodies? But I was nineteen, and I had no answer except that Mary's gift of seeing into the heart of others was a rare and precious thing, and something unknown to me.

On my solo train ride home later that week, I mused over everything I'd seen and heard during my visit. I was sad to hear that Mary's relationship with Al was on hold indefinitely and probably over.

Apparently, they had quite different and incompatible expectations of each other and of their own future careers. But Mary was optimistic about her future, and in the meantime, she loved her job as a nurse at Tranquille School.

8
MATSQUI INSTITUTION, MATSQUI, B.C.

THE FOLLOWING YEAR, THE TRAJECTORY of Mary's life took on a new and exciting, yet ominous direction.

Seeking to broaden her experiences, Mary decided to resign from her nursing position at Tranquille to take up a new posting at the brand-new Matsqui Institution, just outside Abbotsford, B.C. Here she would be working with an entirely different demographic—federal prison inmates.

Unique in the history of the Canadian penitentiary system, the Matsqui Institution was a medium-security prison eighty kilometres from downtown Vancouver. It embodied a new vision for corrections in Canada, with a focus on the treatment of drug addicts in the federal correctional system. As a psychiatric nurse and counsellor, Mary would be working directly with inmates at the Regional Psychiatric Centre.[6]

It was to be a challenging yet exciting opportunity.

It was here at Matsqui that Mary would begin to understand the relationship between mental health and criminality, the nature of addictive behaviour, the role of education as a transformative power for the incarcerated, the role the community could play in assisting the inmate to rehabilitate, and the role that prison culture itself played in creating, magnifying, and often prolonging mental health problems in inmates.

---

6   Renamed the Pacific Institution.

Also working at this medium-security prison was a young classification officer, Mae Burrows,[7] who describes her time with Mary:

> *It was at Matsqui I met Mary Steinhauser. She was young and beautiful with long black hair, a lovely warm smile and a stylish sense of dressing. You could immediately feel her strength and kindness. We became friends as a result of car-pooling to Matsqui from Vancouver.*
>
> *The sixties and seventies were a time of social unrest in Canada, with the rise of feminism, environmentalism, radical politics and a focus on social justice. Prominent on the social justice screen was the emergence of aboriginal rights, the American Indian Movement, and the "genocide in Canada" from residential schools and displacement from traditional lands. Injustices in the legal justice system resulted in a disproportionate number of native men populating Canadian jails.*
>
> *Another surge of political activity was the prisoner's rights movement, birthed from the inhuman conditions in many Canadian jails. Some people worked outside the system on these issues, others worked inside.*
>
> *Mary was a beacon-of-light inside the prison. A classification officer's job was to counsel inmates, make recommendations for employment and education, and work with prisoners to develop pre-release and rehabilitation programs. Unfortunately, it never felt like all prison staff was working toward the same goals. In the adversarial and dichotomized prison culture, where guards were focused on "keeping order," and counselors were focused on rehabilitation, there was an inevitable conflict at both the systems and personal levels.*

---

7   Jennifer Moreau, "Meet Mae: she challenges the status quo," *Burnaby Now*, June 14, 2013, https://www.burnabynow.com/news/meet-mae-she-challenges-the-status-quo-1.407865.

Entering the harsh, metallic, rigid environment of a prison was an assault on the soul and spirit. Matsqui was a relatively new, medium-security prison and Mary was one of a number of well-intentioned, humanistic staff who genuinely believed most inmates could move on to healthier lives.

Mary was a leader in developing and encouraging programs with this intention. There was an "Outsider's Group" of people from the outside who would meet, discuss and socialize with inmates. In Mary's view and in ours, having an opportunity to be with "normal" people was an uplifting and important highlight of an inmate's week and good for his rehabilitation.

There was also a "Wives Group" of inmate's wives and girlfriends who visited weekly. They participated in discussions about family issues. They also took part in therapy sessions—Transactional Analysis was all the rage then. The groups provided inmates with insight, communication skills and social contact. They stood in stark contrast to the intense maleness, rigid routines and the linear, harsh discipline of prison life.

Even giving an inmate a "pass," like a child allowed to walk in the hallway at school was a relief and joy to look forward to for many inmates. When a classification officer, nurse or other personnel had an appointment with an inmate, they would send a pass to walk to their office. Even this short walk would be a break from the relentless routines in jail. Mary issued many passes. Prisoners came to appreciate her compassion, insights, advice on survival skills and hope for the future. But other staff—some guards didn't like these fellows getting their passes.

The rigidity and potentially violent and domineering culture that inevitably takes shape when many men are locked up together for years, was bad enough. What was worse was the threat of being thrown in "the hole"—solitary confinement. Isolating a person from human contact is one of the cruelest things we can do to him. And it is worse when isolation is meted out vindictively.

Mary reacted strongly to such cruelty. She used her strategic, gritty smarts wherever she could to prevent, ameliorate or shorten a prisoner's time in "the hole."

Mary and I lived in Vancouver so Matsqui was a long drive. We'd meet in east Vancouver, edge our car through the dense traffic through town, along the Trans Canada, over the bridge to Surrey and finally the cars would start thinning out, and the beautiful Fraser Valley would open up to us. In those days, Langley and Abbotsford were rural communities and we'd drive past cows and farms and see the lovely mountains cupping this primal valley before we hit the jail.

We had a great time car-pooling. We would rage and rejoice about our day, talk politics and listen and sing along to music on the radio.

Mary was older and wiser than I; my mentor. We shared values and analysis of the situation. We were both determined to make a better world, but Mary was so admirably brave in her resolve to do so.

Coincidentally, around the same time in 1965, a new development was unfolding high up on top of Burnaby Mountain, named after Burnaby, the sprawling suburb just east of Vancouver. The fledgling institution would soon play a pivotal role in Mary's life.

It was the opening of Simon Fraser University.

9
EDUCATED

IT WAS A RARE OCCASION when Mary was influenced by anything I said or did. Three years my senior, she was always the sibling who led the way, set the pace, and decided in which direction we would move. And for the most part, I willingly followed.

Not that I was without conviction or strong beliefs of my own, but Mary was more experienced and had greater social ease to handle situations. For the most part, it was just easier to follow her lead. When she left home to begin her nursing career, I found a greater appetite for putting myself out there, to take charge, to put my own mark on the world around me.

So, at an important juncture in my sister's life, I played a crucially important role in her next life decision.

The year was 1967, and I'd just finished my third semesters at Simon Fraser University in Burnaby, B.C. Just two years old and bursting with a raw youthful energy and passion, SFU, as it came to be known, was a brash upstart in the post-secondary landscape of B.C. in the 1960s. One of its unique drawing cards was a new category of admission, that of the "mature" student, twenty-five years and over, who could be admitted with a lower GPA but would get additional soft credit for work/life experiences as predictors of success in their chosen programs. This relaxing of formerly stringent requirements was very attractive to potential students who had a job and/or families to support and wanted to improve their status in their respective workplace, change careers, or obtain an advanced degree for personal satisfaction.

As for me, university life was so exciting, so exhilarating, and so enchanting, I could hardly believe such a feeling was possible. Every day I was challenged to think, to criticize, to imagine, and to create. My professors' lectures were brilliant, provocative, and thoughtful. Led by bright young graduate students, our small-group tutorials were similarly interesting and engaging.

I was awed, inspired, and in a constant state of fevered excitement.

I knew that Mary would love the university environment as much as I did and understand how a degree would open up so many more opportunities for her in the future. So I set about to persuade her to register at SFU for the fall semester. She finally agreed, and in due course we joined forces with two other women friends to rent a duplex in East Vancouver and share our living costs.

In September 1967, Mary, now twenty-five, proudly registered as a full-time student in the BA program at SFU, majoring in psychology. With her considerable work experience and knowledge of psychiatric nursing and addictions counselling, her chosen major was a supremely appropriate fit for her background.

There was one glitch in our carefully laid plans for Mary's first semester at SFU—she wouldn't be getting much help from me in her first semester at university. I was now going into my fourth semester, but my grades were faltering. I was fatigued and flat broke, so decided to take the semester off from school and do some office temp work for a local police station.

From the get-go, Mary's drive, intensity of focus, and dedication to her studies was astounding. University was serious business for her. As a mature student, she felt she had no time to waste, that every day mattered, and that she had to apply herself with absolute dedication to the task at hand.

In her first semester, I hardly ever saw her. Her weekly schedule was gruelling. She left early in the morning and returned home late at night. On the weekends, she allowed herself an extra hour of sleep in the morning, then she would pack up her books and spend the rest of the day studying in the library at SFU. When she did stay home, she talked about her courses, her profs, the other students, her first impressions of the university, her pending assignments, and essays and projects, which all seemed to be unending.

Sometimes she asked me to type her essays, which I did. Usually good naturedly.

We struck a bargain. Since I had the only typewriter in the house and could type an impressive eighty words-per-minute. I would type Mary's essays; in return, because she owned the only car in the household, she'd do the driving to SFU, pay for gas, and pick up groceries or large items that we couldn't carry home on the bus.

When January came, I started back at SFU, and from that time until I graduated in August of '69 and left B.C., Mary and I lived together, studied together, partied with friends, laughed often, quarrelled frequently, debated continuously, and shared all the ups and downs of student life.

For those two years when our lives were so enmeshed, I'm so grateful and know one thing for sure: I could not be speaking as confidently about the essence of Mary's character and ambitions, about her motivations for her actions and her choices, and about the crusading spirit she came to be without that time together. Several facets of her character are forever unknowable to me, but for the most part, I came to know my sister as well as anyone ever could have.

Our daily schedule was set by Mary, who being the owner of a shiny red Corvair, possessed the sole means of transportation in our household. At around 7:00 a.m. on weekday mornings, Mary's alarm, or more precisely alarms, jolted us awake with their incessant rings. Because Mary slept so soundly, she set two alarm clocks, one ten minutes later than the other, in two separate places in her bedroom, both just out of reach of her bed. When the first one rang, she'd leap out of bed, grab it off its shelf, quickly turn it off, and then jump back into bed for the next few minutes of precious sleep before the second one rang.

Then our morning ritual would begin.

We were always trying to save money, so on most days we made our own lunches. They were very spartan—Rye Crisp crackers, cheese, and a piece of fruit. Sometimes if we had money to splurge, we'd get a hamburger and fries in the cafeteria, but Mary was very careful with her money and didn't often indulge.

Most mornings, we jumped into the car setting out eastbound on 41st Avenue until we reached Boundary Road and then north down the Boundary Road hill, where in front of us, the snow-capped magnificence of the North Shore Mountains gradually appeared as we descended. On clear, crisp, winter mornings, the breathtaking panorama was especially stunning. In minutes we were travelling eastbound the the freeway until we reached Gaglardi Way and began the steep ascent up to the campus on top of the mountain.

We'd set off to our separate classes: Mary to lectures or tutorials in psychology, sociology, political science, anthropology, and English, and me to geography, English, French, and philosophy.

In all the time we were at university, we didn't take any classes together, but we studied together most days. We would sometimes meet throughout the day, and always after five in the smoking lounge on the second floor of the library, by this time blue with smoke. Since we were smokers, this suited us fine. Often, if there were a seat at the same table, we'd sit across from one another.

After a full day of classes and tutorials, by 6:00 p.m. I was itching to go home, but Mary always insisted on staying to study in the lounge until 9:30 or 10:00 p.m. She was so determined to succeed that she drove herself almost to exhaustion. I'd look across at her face as she pored over her books; often she was pale and fatigued.

Sometimes, I'd plead with her to go home early, but she'd say she had more work to do and we'd have to stay. So after many such entreaties, ignored or declined, I gave up asking and resigned myself to the fact that we'd be staying every night until late, at least on weekdays.

Although initially I resented this gruelling schedule, I used my time wisely during those long days and evenings in the library. At the end of that first semester, something truly amazing happened. My grades shot up to new heights, and they stayed there until I graduated.

Without a doubt, I owe Mary a great deal for her insistence that we make the best use of our collective time. She pushed us both to work diligently, and her dogged determination was not just to succeed, but to excel.

But Mary wasn't all work and no play.

On Saturday nights, we'd frequently cut loose. clubbing or going to movies with friends. Mary loved to dance, throwing herself with complete abandon into the joy of moving to music. She also liked the pub atmosphere and loved sitting around drinking beer and talking with friends about ideas, projects, university politics, and topics of the day. Some weekends we'd have parties at our place, sometimes drinking too much and suffering the inevitable hangover the next day.

It was all so much fun. Life throbbed with promise and excitement.

During the late '60s, SFU was a hotbed of political activity. The epicentre of student protests was the main mall, where mass meetings were often called for the noon hour. The topics were generally about some aspect of student life that was being debated, some authority that was being challenged, or some action that needed to be voted on. These meetings could go on for hours. But with every motion, countermotion, and vote, each of us had to think about the issue, decide for ourselves what we should do, and finally decide how to vote. Sometimes we were challenged in this way on a daily basis. Our discussions bled into the classrooms, and like it or not, our teaching assistants and profs would often get involved in dialogue with their classes about the issue at hand.

On one occasion, the SFU Student Society rallied the troops to occupy the administration building in protest of some administrative action or inaction. Because Mary was taking sociology, and profs in that department were much more politically minded, she was more interested in taking part in protests than I. She decided to join the sit-in and asked me if I'd like to come and have a look, so I did. Students were sitting on the floor, leaning against the walls in the corridors and mostly talking. Not much was happening; still, I was a reluctant observer and unwilling to risk getting arrested by the RCMP who it was rumoured they were eventually going to be called in to clean out all these unruly, longhaired student protestors. With that in mind I soon left, and eventually Mary did, too.

By August 1969, I'd finished all my coursework. With my newly minted BA in hand, I got married to a fellow student; bade farewell to B.C., Mary, our mom and dad, and my friends; and moved to Toronto to begin the next chapter in my life. It was one rich in experience and growth in many ways, but one in which I'd never again enjoy the same level of intimacy with my big sister as I enjoyed in those intensely euphoric university years.

From that time on, we communicated by letter or infrequently by phone, because long distance calls in those days were very expensive. On at least three occasions over the next five-year period, I returned to B.C. to visit our parents and Mary, who still had a way to go to finish up at SFU.

It was during one of these summer semesters that Mary met Helen Potrebenko,[8] also a mature student and budding writer, who describes her time with Mary:

> *I only knew Mary Steinhauser for one summer and I don't know what year that was—most likely 1970 although it may have been 1971 or 1969. Since I was taking sociology and Mary, psychology, I don't know how I met her as I did not tend to be friendly with psychology types. Probably we just started sitting together at the Simon Fraser Pub because we were both older women students. Mary had been a nurse and I had been a lab technician; that seems like a lot to have in common among a sea of young students.*
>
> *In one of our early conversations, Mary told me she was feeding the pigeons. She was taking a course in behavioural psychology and they were doing some kind of deprivation experiment with pigeons. Mary did not, of course, believe that these were necessary so she went to the lab at night and fed the pigeons. I don't know if she told anyone else or if the professors knew why their experiments didn't work.*
>
> *The other pub conversations were probably about the men who found Mary attractive. Some tall professor named R. or something followed her around eagerly, telling her among other things, that his wife didn't understand him. He was a very silly person. Mary was polite to him but always burst into giggles after she had shaken him off.*

---

8   BC Booklook, "#82 Helen Potrebenko," bio of the B.C. author, January 26, 2016, https://bcbooklook.com/2016/01/26/82-helen-potrebenko/.

We would not have talked much about politics because among the hotbed of revolutionary talk, neither of us were proper radicals. Mary was very practical and simply ignored ideology and its correctness. She laughed a lot. She seemed not to find ideas of overwhelming importance and thought what people did was far more important than what they thought. But we were both greatly affected by the events at Simon Fraser and all the SFU radicals knew her and some of them hung out at her place. Probably they were drawn by her compassionate nature.

It must have been 1970, the year after many of the professors were fired. That the student rebellion was over wasn't obvious at the time because of all the frantic activity going on. I went to the pub because everybody went to the pub and assume that Mary went for the same reason. It was all frantic and fascinating although nothing was really happening except for power games for the professors. Mary and I were bemused by it all and it sometimes seemed to me that she and I were the only sane people around. Mary was known as a "bleeding heart," a dismissive phrase to downgrade kindness and compassion in a society where cruelty and greed are rewarded.

By the end of December 1970, Mary had completed all her coursework. After eight consecutive semesters at SFU, she had achieved her BA (Honours) in both Psychology and Sociology with a GPA of 3.70.

How proud and gratified she felt!

Now it was time to set in motion the next stage in her professional journey. Over that year, Mary had been considering various plans for her future. Her intention was to further her education towards a career that would combine her training and experience in mental health, her desire to help those most in need in society, and her scholarly ambitions. To that end, all her instincts, drives, and ambitions to serve and support those most in need in society were met in one profession—that of a social worker.

They all coalesced at one point on the horizon: the School of Social Work at the University of British Columbia, the only post-secondary institution in B.C. to offer a Master of Social Work degree.

It was September 1971 when Mary began her studies at UBC, the sprawling campus of Western Canada's largest, oldest, and most prestigious university, set in the middle of an old-growth forest on Vancouver's west side. It was an exciting time, and she threw herself into her first-year studies.

In her journey to educate herself, one gnawing, ever-present issue for Mary was the necessity to earn money while she was attending university. Going into debt was the absolute worst fate Mary could imagine, and she steadfastly refused to take out any kind of student loan or borrow money from anyone—not even our parents—to fund her university studies.

If need be, she was determined to work full time to fund her studies and avoid any lingering debt.

Fortunately, as an experienced psychiatric nurse, Mary was well positioned to work in mental health settings. Throughout her last year at SFU and for the duration of her program at UBC, she worked full or part time in the psychiatric unit of the Lions Gate Hospital in North Vancouver. Often this was a graveyard shift, which meant remaining awake and alert all night and then driving to campus, attending classes, and falling into bed in the late afternoon, only to rise again after only a few hours' sleep to get ready for her midnight start time at the hospital.

It was a punishing schedule.

Nevertheless, Mary persevered, and toward the end of her second year, she began work on her thesis, "Single Professional Women in Retirement." Around this time, I asked Mary why she was interested in researching single professional women in retirement. What, in particular, I wondered, drove her to examine this issue?

"Well," she replied, "I'll probably end up single…and I want to find out how other single career women feel about their lives once they've retired."

It was 1973, and Mary was thirty-one years old.

For some time, Mary had believed it was unlikely that she was ever going to "settle down" and get married or have children. Not that she lacked for male partners, friends, and suitors. As a tall, strikingly pretty and charming woman, she was an intensely interesting speaker and could hold a group in thrall with her stories and theories about various social justice issues. She was also immensely sociable and cheerful, and loved having a good time.

Of little interest to her, however, was the domestic life of a wife and mother. She believed that a husband would expect at least some domestic commitment from her, some interest or skill in cooking, cleaning, household management, personal attention, and quite possibly, the expectation to bear children. In all the time we spent together as children or adults, Mary had never once expressed any desire to have children. This scenario wasn't even remotely in Mary's universe.

She even spoke with wicked irony about her "hopeless" chest, a spin on the traditional hope chest, that storage chest of our generation which young women carefully stocked with linens, china, towels, sheets, silverware, glassware, and tablecloths, all in the expectation of a blissful married life.

It seemed Mary's prospect of getting married was, year by year, becoming less likely. With her busy schedule, how would she find time to look after a home or a husband, or even considering adding children to the picture?

She found it far more exhilarating to be studying or working in the intense environments of hospitals and prisons, especially now that she would be in a position to create or make policies about social justice issues. In those environments, she could make real and meaningful change.

So most likely, she was destined to be a single woman in her retirement. But would she be happy, or lonely, bitter, and disappointed with life? Weren't all single women unhappy in their old age? Would such a dismal fate be hers, too, at the end of life? What better way to find out than to make this troubling area of concern the object of her enquiry!

We talked about what she expected her findings to reveal. Mary was open about her bias, fully expecting that the majority of the respondents would be mostly unsatisfied and unhappy with their lives…After all, she opined as an aside, isn't that what the stereotype of the aging spinster—unfulfilled, dried up, abandoned, and alone—suggests?

Her findings, however, revealed something quite unexpected.

In the abstract to her Master's thesis, "Single Professional Women in Retirement,"[9] Mary described the purpose of the study: to identify the needs of single women in retirement as to income, housing, health, social and recreational activities, and interpersonal relationships; the need for appropriate pre-retirement programs; and further knowledge of the current availability of programs and services. To this end, she interviewed sixty-two single professional women, aged fifty-seven to seventy-eight, who had retired within the last two years and were living in the Lower Mainland. This sample consisted of seventeen nurses, twenty-four teachers, twelve social workers, five businesswomen, and four women classified as miscellaneous.

To her amazement, and quite at odds with Mary's initial bias, the happiness factor of single professional women in retirement was found to be overwhelmingly positive. In her summary and conclusions, she writes:

> *The overall impression gained from the study is that this group of single retired professional women are leading meaningful and satisfying lives. Their single status appears to have contributed significantly to their ability to be independent throughout their lives as well as in retirement...*
>
> *In addition, retirement, if viewed from the perspective of the majority of these women can be a most pleasant experience.*[10]

What an incredibly proud day it was for our family when we heard the news that Mary's thesis had been accepted, earning her a first-class standing, and that her standing for her entire two-year course of study at UBC was also first class.

Six years had passed since the beginning of her exciting, euphoric, and intensely challenging journey through academia. But now, a new and much darker chapter in Mary's life was about to be written.

---

9   Mary Steinhauser, "Single professional women in retirement," (Master's thesis, University of British Columbia, 1973), vi, http://resolve.library.ubc.ca/cgi-bin/catsearch?bid=1560712.

10 Steinhauser, "Single professional women," 75.

10
THE PEN

Silken Halo

Silken halo of midnight hair...
Frames her face, lovely, fair.
It falls upon her soft white shoulders,
Is a waterfall...upon the boulders.
Tumbling, cascading to her breasts,
Not to die but there to rest,
Then kiss each breast with silken tress,
Like velvet midnight...the stars caress.

You're still a wondrous butterfly ---,
But beware of nets!

Much love,
Anonymous

A poem written for Mary
by a B.C. Penitentiary inmate,
October 15, 1974

It was in October of 1973 that Mary landed her very first job after graduating with a Master's of Social Work from UBC. Not a traditional job for a newbie social worker, to be sure, but a permanent position nonetheless paying a decent annual salary of $11,746 plus benefits—good news for a young woman weary of six long years of student penury and self-sacrifice. Interesting and challenging, too, the position offered opportunities to effect real change in the lives of many.

Her job title was "classification officer." Her clients were male inmates who had sentences of at least two years plus a day, and her workplace was the British Columbia Penitentiary,[11] one of the most dangerous and violent maximum-security prisons in all of Canada. Mary was aware that the "Pen" had been described in unflattering terms as medieval in design and function. Opened in 1878 and located high above the Fraser River in New Westminster, B.C. on 65.5 acres, the penitentiary's gothic buildings, with guard towers at each corner, resembled a medieval castle fortress. This impression was further enhanced by the 9.14 metres (30 feet) high concrete wall that completely surrounded it.

Mary didn't mind, though. After months of job hunting, she'd finally obtained a well-paying position in an area of criminology that suited her qualifications; she would be working closely with inmates in a variety of ways. As a classification officer (referred to today as an institutional parole officer), Mary had many responsibilities. On her caseload were sixty inmates. Her primary duties and responsibilities were:

1. The development of a program plan, upon the admission of a new inmate, which best suited the needs of the individual within the available facilities and resources of the institution. This included interviews and analysis of available data to determine the individual's security status, vocational, psychiatric, psychological, and academic needs, etc. A report was prepared and referrals were submitted as required to the appropriate departments.

2. Individual counselling of approximately sixty inmates, including the preparation of progress reports, transfer reports, and other reports as required.

---

11   Established in 1878, the B.C. Penitentiary was a federal maximum security prison situated in New Westminster, British Columbia, Canada. After 102 years in operation, it was decommissioned in 1980. It was the first federal penal institution in Western Canada.

3. Presentation of cases to the Regional Classification Board for consideration for reduced security, as well as organizing and attending case conferences on inmates.

4. Pre-parole and pre-release planning on behalf of inmates, including using and liaising with institutional and community resources.

5. Presentation of cases for temporary absences, return of statutory remission, work changes, etc., and preparation of replies to queries from outside agencies and individuals regarding inmates.

6. Maintaining good working relationships with other institutional departments, federal and provincial institutions, various public and private agencies, and inmates (the latter included supervising visits between inmates and families).[12]

At the time she began work at the Pen, Mary was sharing the Main Street duplex with a sensitive young woman named Penny. Mary was a great talker, and if she had an audience, she could dissertate for hours on any topic that interested her. Her new job at the penitentiary fascinated her, and so Penny was compelled to listen as Mary explored and examined each and every facet of her employment there. At times, Penny's attention would lapse, and her thoughts drift off to other concerns only to be interrupted by Mary's query, "Don't you think so, Penny?"

But Mary had a way of making people listen. Perhaps it was the intensity of her devotion to her job, her obvious sincerity, or the manner in which she related events that captured the imagination. In any event, it was impossible to be with Mary without being drawn into her world.

As Penny writes in her narrative of Mary's time in the B.C. Penitentiary:

> *From the first day, she needed to talk about her work when she got home. The work intrigued her because she was a crusader yet it also stifled her with its bureaucracy.*

---

12 From M. Franz private papers.

Mary very seldom, if ever, judged people as being totally beyond hope. She was capable of breaking the barriers of fear often found between the free person and the prisoner. Perhaps this was due in part to having previously worked in institutions for the mentally ill. But it was due also to her own special genius for reaching out to people on an equal level and her supreme faith in human nature. She was not the kind of person who needed to feel superior by putting neither her fellow man down, nor the kind that took any sadistic pleasure in seeing people locked up or turning the key behind them.

Newspapers place much drama onto institutions and the violence of their inmates yet for all that Mary was frequently alone without a guard among prisoners: murderers, addicts, etc., in a room where she conducted group therapy in a democratic fashion. She placed much hope on the efforts of the group and her grocery list included coffee, sugar and cream for the gatherings.

There were many things she talked about in regard to the prison structure, but certain themes were recurring in her conversations.

The atmosphere she said was so thick with hate you could cut it with a knife. She was referring to the total structure, not just the inmates. There was a hierarchy among the prisoners. Some of the prisoners had so much power that even the guards were afraid, thus enabling them to get privileges sooner than others. It was a chauvinistic hierarchy with many of the prisoners and the staff believing that women should not be hired in prisons. She often felt buffeted from every side, although she was generally well liked and respected among the inmates.

She was adamantly against capital punishment, not only because she did not believe in taking a person's life, legal or not, but she said statistics proved that capital punishment was not a deterrent to crime and also it cost the taxpayer more to execute than it did to incarcerate for life.

She took her work very seriously and never missed a day. Every night and weekend she brought files home to work on. She was concerned about the prisoners on her caseload as individuals. She seldom mentioned names but she would talk about cases.

The injustice of the sentence of a native prisoner who was convicted for stealing two steaks.

The young man who desperately wanted to get transferred because of homosexual advances from other prisoners.

The man who got drunk and awakened with a murder charge yet could remember nothing.

The older prisoner who befriended her and tried to help her in her work by advising her about some of the facts of prison life.

The prisoners and ex-inmates who sent her cards and letters.

One such letter is from J.B., an inmate at Matsqui Institution. October 18, 1974

Dear Mary,

Hello, how is my favourite classification officer? I was thinking I should come back to the Penitentiary just so I could talk to you again.

This institution, I think, is fairly good as far as a prison goes. You have so much time on your hands. You actually have to look for something to do. I have joined the Gavel Club, JC's and participated in a few AA meetings. Speaking of AA, the liaison officer for the club and I used to drink together for a number of years. We both have been off the bottle for almost 2 years. It was quite a touching sight when we first spied one another.

> *Since I have been here I have gained approximately 8 pounds. The food is much better and most of the time you have a choice of different meals.*
>
> *In case you happen to be out this way, please do drop in. I have you on my approved visiting list. I would enjoy seeing you again.*
>
> *Well, its beddy-bye time, so I'll say nighty-night for now.*
>
> Love,
J.B.

Eight months later, in a letter to the editor of the *Vancouver Sun*, this same inmate writes:

Sir—Mary Steinhauser likes people so much that "she gave everyone a chance." This was your leading line in a front page article in the Sun on June 14. Oh, how true that statement was.

> *Mary helped many inmates when others had given up on them as hopeless cases. Why she helped us, we all knew—she just loved helping people, especially people in extreme need. How she helped them when others failed, we'll never know. Perhaps it was the way she had about her—her true concern for others.*
>
> *I know this because I was one of such difficult inmates.*
>
> *...*
>
> *It will be a long time for many, many inmates before they forget the help that Mary was able to give to them. There will never be another person who has helped so many inmates.*
>
> *May God put Mary at a special place by his side.*
> *J.B.*

Some years later, in his narrative entitled, "*I was doing a ten-year stretch for armed robbery,*" an ex-inmate describes the profound effect Mary had on him during and after he served his time at the Pen.

I was a "resident" at the B.C. Pen from 1973 to 1975. I had just turned 23 having never been in jail before. I was shifted onto Mary's caseload by my former classification officer. I was doing a ten year stretch for armed robbery. This may appear somewhat disjointed but I'm muddling through. I was a young, stupid and angry young man, passionate and principled but without malice and had never hurt another human being with the exception of supremely disappointing my mother and family and robbing a store. I can't begin to tell you what a hellish place this was. This Penitentiary. It was built in 1888. I digress. Mary came to my rescue and made it possible for me to move on. She saw my naiveté (not my innocence) and recognized I had to get out of this place. She arranged my transfer to Matsqui.

...

I imagine that soldiers who survive combat suffer from PTS syndrome. For the little more than two years I resided there I saw so many cruel and vicious deaths and was many times in the proximity of the saddest suicides.

Sometimes I think I endure rather than say I survived. To this day I strive to be half the person Mary was. I'll never forget her.

Name withheld

"Mary was my angel. She rescued me from the dark depths of a cell in solitary confinement." So begins a more recent compilation of short emails from a former inmate of the B.C. Penitentiary in New Westminster. Ironically, he had started out as a prison guard but somehow went astray and ended up in prison himself.

However, his life took a dramatic turn for the better, and eventually he managed to reclaim his life. He wishes to remain anonymous, but not silent. Now in his seventies, after a long and good life, he remembers:

In 1967 when I was 18, I became a prison guard in

Quebec where I worked for five years. I bought a nice home and a new car—life looked pretty good.

But after a few years, the heavy mortgage and car payments were more than I could handle. I was desperate. I needed to find extra cash in a hurry. It started with a series of hold-ups. But an incident happened, and without giving all the details, I can honestly say I've regretted it for the rest of my life. Even before being convicted, I recognized and faced my guilt...and had to prepare myself to do time...a lot of time.

And so, at the age of 23, I found myself behind bars. I was eventually moved to the BC Pen where it looked like I'd be serving the rest of my twenty-five year sentence. I spent most of my time regretting what I'd done.

In prison, violence was routine: often from prisoners, and yes, even from the guards. Nothing ever seemed to change. More than once, I ended up in "the hole" in solitary confinement. Strangely, the "hole" at the BC Pen was known as the "Penthouse" but, I assure you, not because of its luxury accommodations. It was indeed a dark and miserable hole—it just happened to occupy a small unit above the cell blocks of one the buildings.

One day, in the Penthouse, I heard a knock at my door. A female voice was offering me educational courses! I couldn't believe my ears. It felt like a light was shining down on me at the bottom of my cell...

It was Mary!

That day I received the biggest light of my life. Her light changed me completely. Instead of drowning in regret for what I'd done, Mary gave me hope in the future. She helped me start putting all that regret behind me. She showed me that I was a person...a person deserving something better than the unhealthy, smothering confines of the hole.

Mary was my angel. She touched my heart. Over the following months, as my classification officer, Mary made many changes that helped me get back on my feet.

It's important to know that back then, Mary faced a deadly cocktail of desperate inmates and scared, angry guards. In this situation, anything can happen. And in a place where nothing seemed to change, she was a change maker.

Today I want to thank Mary Steinhauser. She rescued me from the depths of a cell in solitary confinement by giving me hope in life itself. Eventually I was able to leave prison on parole. I was completely rehabilitated back into society and I've lived well for many years.

I have kept my promises to her...she will stay in my heart forever.

Name withheld

11
41 HOURS

She was too close to the fire
Burning in the cell blocks
Steinhauser classification officer
Was devoured in the system
In the secret holes of bureaucracy
A hundred thousand dusty guys
Were filed away in her screams

—From a poem entitled "Hostage"
unsigned[13]

THE FIRST MORNING ALARM SHATTERED the early stillness in the duplex at 5887 Main Street. It was 7:00 a.m. on Monday, June 9, and the young woman, with her mass of dark and tangled hair, moved restlessly in her bed. She reached out, groping for the button on the radio alarm clock to quiet the unwelcome sound. Serenity was restored. Sighing, she snuggled more deeply under the blankets. At 7:05 a.m., a second alarm rent the air, provoking an immediate response from the woman, now half awake.

She swung her legs out onto the floor, displacing the dozing cat at the end of her bed. "Sorry, Corkie," she mumbled, pushing the hair out of her

---

13 Judith Timson, "Steinhauser: Was she killed by B.C.'s jail system?" *Toronto Star*, January 26, 1976, A6.

face while making her way to the bathroom where she spent the next ten minutes getting ready for work.

After a breakfast of black coffee, hard-boiled eggs, and toast, she fed the meowing cat. Pulling on her blue suede jacket, she took one last look in the mirror to check that her make-up was properly applied. On her way out the back door to her parked car, she grabbed her black vinyl briefcase, bulging with miscellaneous papers, confidential case files, and dozens of pens, pencils, and erasers.

Although the car was still chilly, the day promised to be a warm one. Inserting her key into the starter, she sighed with relief as the engine kicked to life. She backed out into the alley behind the duplex, continuing on for a block, then turned right and eased into the southbound traffic down to Marine Drive.

It was 7:25 a.m. and Mary Steinhauser, prison classification officer, was on her way to work at the British Columbia Penitentiary in New Westminster, B.C.

As she drove, she thought about the week before. Last Friday had been a difficult day. An inmate named Andy had been in her office for about an hour. He was getting up to leave when he said, "What if I refuse to go?" He stood there waiting for Mary to respond. After an awkward silence, Mary replied, "Well, there's nothing much I can do about it, I guess."

The remark nagged at her throughout the weekend, and she'd fretted about it with Penny. "I don't know anything for sure," Mary said, "but I just feel that something's going to happen out there."

"Well, for God's sake, Mary, don't go to work then," Penny pleaded. "You've got lots of sick time built up. Why don't you take Monday off?"

"I can't do that," she sighed. "I've got too much work to do."

Although Andy hadn't been on Mary's caseload, he'd been working quite closely with her as the secretary of the Community Awareness Group, a group of inmates who, with Mary's guidance, came together to plan, organize, and implement social events at the Pen for friends, community leaders, and relatives from the outside. Born in North Vancouver, Andy Bruce, twenty-six years old, was a "lifer." In April 1970, already working as a contract killer, he murdered a dancer receiving one ounce of heroin as payment for the job. In August 1972, he was transferred to the Saskatchewan Penitentiary for disciplinary reasons. While there, he attempted to escape, stabbing one officer and holding another officer as hostage.[14]

But Mary was a penitentiary social worker, and Andy's record of offences wouldn't have concerned her overly much. None of the inmates on her caseload had pasts that were pure or untainted. Her job as a classification officer was to support and help the inmate so that, upon release, his future wouldn't resemble his past.

In some strange, inexplicable way, Mary felt an affinity for Andy. He seemed to possess some magnetism, a measure of dynamism and energy that many other inmates lacked. Although she knew he was a lifer, she felt he could be particularly useful as a spokesperson for the Aboriginal inmate population. In fact, as the current chairman of the Native Brotherhood at the penitentiary, she saw that Andy could potentially be of great value as a role model, mentor, and even a leader in the Aboriginal community, both while finishing out his prison sentence and once he'd been paroled. Because of his youth and his intellectual abilities, Mary felt there was a chance for him to understand and appreciate the factors that had brought him to the penitentiary. With that insight, he might realize that a more purposeful, worthwhile life existed for him on the outside. There was good reason for optimism about Andy Bruce, Mary felt.

Their meetings were often fraught with tension, however. Andy resented the fact that it was Mary who had the choice of requesting to see him. It was she who had to fill out the official "pass" that would bring him to her. He particularly resented the fact that, as a woman and as a classification officer, Mary held the upper hand. She called all the shots.

They discussed, on occasion, the changing role of women and the women's liberation movement. In their discussions, Mary made it very clear that she considered herself a truly liberated woman and she felt that male chauvinism was a very real and tangible presence in the Pen; the staff seemed to feel that the female classification officers had an easier time of it, and the inmates regarded the female COs as sexual objects or "easy marks." No one saw them as real professionals whose purpose was to help the inmates in their efforts to become rehabilitated and eventually released. In

---

14 "Murder charges stayed against B.C. Pen three," newspaper article, n.p., n.d.

the male-dominated world of the B.C. Penitentiary, both keeper and kept shared the same point of view: women were definitely out of place, and their presence was merely tolerated.

For a dedicated professional such as Mary, who took great pride in her work, this was a difficult pill to swallow. Mary could be faulted perhaps by her superiors for her "liberal" views or for her failure to uphold strict institutional policies in matters such as security, but few employees in that organization could match her work ethic, dedication, and enthusiasm. Her work was her life. She had none of the usual family obligations to distract her, and every evening and on weekends, she would bring files home to work on.

She was far too conscientious to take time off without actually being sick, and so she brushed off Penny's suggestion that she take the day off. But still, she fretted as she drove along Columbia Street and turned into the entrance to the penitentiary grounds. She wondered what it would be like to be taken hostage, how she would feel, and how the administration at the Pen would react.

"Ah," she chastised her anxious self, "don't worry. Nothing will happen. You're making a mountain out of a molehill."

Passing through the front gates of the penitentiary, Mary said, "Good morning," to the security stationed there and then made her way through the courtyard and up the steps into the Classification Building, a frame structure about 20 feet wide and 220 feet long. She walked into Room 201 at the entrance and saw the custodial officer sitting there.

"Hi," she said. "How're you?"

"Pretty good," he replied. "How're you?"

Before she had a chance to answer, John Ryan, another classification officer, called down from his office. "Hey, Mary, want to have a look at the pictures I took of the Community Awareness thing?"

As she turned to walk down the corridor, out of the corner of her eye she saw the figure of Andy Bruce. "Morning, Andy," she said lightly and, without waiting for a reply, continued down to her office.

"Come into my office, John; let's look at them in here."

It had been two weeks before, on May 29, that an inmate planning committee hosted a social gathering of about a hundred people at the Pen. The attendees were the inmates, their family and friends, several staff members and selected community leaders. As the secretary of the group, Andy had worked very hard on the planning and staffing of the event. Among the guests was his uncle, Chief Dan George, the renowned Aboriginal patriarch of the Squamish Nation. Chief George had famously achieved stardom in Hollywood for his 1969 role in the film *Little Big Man*, playing alongside Dustin Hoffman. He was nominated for Best Supporting Actor that year.

The gathering was a great success. John, as the designated event photographer, had shot an entire film roll on his camera, capturing comrades in twos and threes and whole groups of smiling guests and inmates, their arms linked and heads inclined in easy friendship. The photos underscored the general feeling of goodwill and amiability that enveloped the group at the party.

A smile spread across Mary's face as she spied the shot John had taken of her, Andy, and Chief Dan George.

"That's a good one!" she cried.

Just then, the sound of scuffling and loud voices came from the hallway. Moments later, the door burst open; in the doorway stood an inmate, gesturing at them with a boning knife.

"Lucas!" John gasped.

In a flash, Dwight Lucas, convicted as an accessory to an axe murder, grabbed John around the throat, pointing the knife at his jugular. He pushed John to exit Mary's office. Lucas turned then and motioned for Mary to precede them down the hallway.

"Get down to the vault!" he screamed.

Mary felt her mouth go dry. What was happening? Was this a hostage-taking? Was it really happening…this thing she'd feared most of all? Stunned, she forced her legs to carry her down the hallway to Room 9. There she saw her colleagues, all classification officers except one, standing about; their eyes were wide with fear and uncertainty.

She tried to quiet the chaos in her mind and ignore the sinking dread that arose in her chest. She looked around at her physical surroundings.

Room 9 was the headquarters for the social and cultural development officers' activities. Entry was made through a Dutch door—so named because it was split in half horizontally, the lower half approximately four feet from the floor, so that the upper half could be opened to allow an unobstructed view into the room while access was restricted by the lower half, which was secured by a lock at about waist level. Not easily accessible from the outside were two additional locks about an inch from the floor. She noticed a sofa, a radio, and a TV in the room.

The corridor wall of Room 9 had three opaque window partitions, one to the right of the Dutch door upon entry to the room and two to the left. Room 9 also had a small sub-office approximately eight by ten feet, with windows about five feet above the floor. This office was located to the right of the Dutch door.

There were sixteen hostages in Room 9: one corrections officer; thirteen classification officers, counting herself; and two social and cultural development officers. There were also three inmates in Room 9. Besides Andy Bruce and Dwight Lucas, there was a third whose name she later learned was Claire Wilson. She recalled, after overhearing his name, that in November '74 he'd been involved in an attack on escorting officers who'd been returning him to the Pen from Nanaimo, where he'd been taken for court hearings.

"All right, which one of you has the key to the vault?" Bruce demanded.

"I do," replied one of the hostages. He was marched out by one of the inmates to his office, where he picked up the key and returned to Room 9.

"Okay, everyone, into the vault!" Bruce commanded in a tone that left no doubt in the minds of the hostages that there would be little to gain by resisting.

"All right, hands on your heads and keep them there!" Lucas shouted once they'd gotten into the vault. The hostages did as they were told and then, one by one, Lucas frisked them. He took away their wallets, rings, and shoes.

They waited silently.

Mary looked around the vault. They had come into it through two doors. The first was a swinging door that moved in an arc from right to left. Immediately behind the swinging door was a steel sliding door without stops at either end. The vault itself was a concrete box-like structure about twelve feet deep and sixteen feet wide. Inside the vault were two rows of shelves in the centre portion and shelves on the two side walls. There were no windows, only ventilation holes. It was being used as a storage room for inactive files and confidential reports.

As she stood, her arms beginning to ache from holding them on her head, Mary recalled someone once telling her that a couple of years before, a classification officer had been taken hostage by two inmates armed with knives. He had been held for about ten hours in this same vault.

My God, she thought, *it's hot in here.*

Just then Andy Bruce, his voice tense and betraying the agitation of recent events, looked directly at Mary and said, "Someone's going to have to be principal hostage."

There was an awkward moment of silence.

Then, very calmly, Mary said, "I will."

She walked towards Andy and he gestured ahead of him. She preceded him out of the vault and back into Room 9, where he motioned to a waiting chair. He quickly moved into position behind her, while holding the butcher knife about an inch from her throat.

Beads of perspiration began to form on Mary's upper lip; her throat felt dry and raspy.

Holy God, what's he going to do? she thought, and fear crept in along the corridors of her mind.

Just then, an official of the penitentiary appeared at the Dutch door, at which point Andy stated their demands. Their principal demand was that a helicopter be provided to take the three hostage-takers and all their hostages to the Vancouver airport, to be flown to a sympathetic foreign country. In addition, they wanted a team of negotiators to assist in negotiations between themselves and the penitentiary administration. Other demands were for drugs, specifically Demerol,[15] a morphine substitute, and restraint equipment for the hostages.

As the morning wore on, various people appeared at the Dutch door, and Bruce was informed that the negotiating team had been assembled.

"That's good," he replied. "Now what about the helicopter?"

---

15 Trade name for meperidine, a narcotic compound used as an analgesic and sedative.

"You know, Bruce," the official replied, "it's going to be pretty hard to get out of the country. Is there any alternative you'd be willing to accept?"

"No way!" Bruce shot back. "Either we leave or we die, and we're going to take the lot with us. If we don't get taken out of the country, heads will roll!"

Mary was convinced he meant every word of it. Her throat tightened, and she swallowed to allay the painful constrictions. Her first thought was that the Canadian Penitentiary Service would never agree to transport inmates to the airport so they could be flown to another country. But if the government didn't agree to the inmates' demands, someone would surely be killed.

I wonder who? she thought. *Will it be me? Would he actually cut my throat after all the hours and days I've spent talking, advising, listening, and working with him? Could he? Would he?*

A cynical voice from within interrupted. *You're expendable, you know. He doesn't give a damn about you, you're just a pawn in a desperate ploy he's making. Even if he has any feelings for you, he won't let it interfere with his plans.*

Furiously, she countered. *But no! I can't believe that! I've never done anything to hurt him. I've only tried to help him—we have a good relationship; he knows that I care about him.*

So what? Do you actually think he cares about you?

Reason and common sense returned.

Don't panic, just don't panic. Don't let anyone see you're frightened! You've been in tight situations before, and you've gotten out of them in one piece. If everyone uses their heads and doesn't panic, then we'll be okay. Try to talk to Andy…defuse the situation. If he sees that you're co-operating with him and won't do anything sudden or unexpected, he might relax a bit.

A nervous, perspiring prison official appeared at the door. "Bruce," he said, "I've got a vial of Demerol and I'll inject you myself or give you a syringe full, but I won't give you the vial."

Andy's eyes narrowed into tiny slits. He screamed, "If you think one lousy vial of Demerol is worth a hostage's life!" and he grabbed Mary more tightly around her shoulders. He made a slicing motion across her exposed throat.

For a moment, Mary's heart stopped. She waited for the first sensation of pain to blot out consciousness.

It never came.

"Okay, okay!" The officer thrust the vial at Andy. "Cool it! You can have it!"

Mary was still trembling as Andy injected her with the Demerol. She dared not look into his face or let him see the terror in her own. She bowed her head and tried to concentrate on the effects of the drug. When it was obvious that Mary wasn't suffering any negative side effects, Andy gave himself a shot. Then he passed the vial, along with the syringe, to Lucas and Wilson, who were in the vault with the fifteen other hostages.

When she saw the immediate crisis was over, Mary began to breathe more regularly again, and her pulse rate returned, more or less, to normal.

Please, God, she pleaded silently, *don't let anyone do anything rash.*

Throughout the day, members of the negotiating team came to the Dutch door and spoke with Andy Bruce about various aspects of their demands. One of the hostages, a prison guard, was released; someone managed to convince Andy that the guard had a heart condition and could die without his medication. A portable toilet was brought in and placed in the small sub-office in Room 9; sandwiches and soft drinks were supplied to the hostages and inmates.

The air in Room 9 was thick with the odour of stale breath and acrid body smells. Nervous tension, coupled with the stifling room temperature, made it difficult to breathe. Mary forced herself to eat the sandwiches that were offered to her but hardly tasted them. It gave her something to do, though, and she thought the food might help to ease the pains in her stomach.

At one point during the afternoon, Mary overheard Lucas ask Andy, "Do you want the women to go and just keep the male hostages?"

Andy then turned to Mary and said, "Do you want to go?"

With only a moment's hesitation, Mary's replied, "No, I'll stay...Let the rest of the people go. Let the two women hostages go, and keep about five of the men, and let the rest go."

At about eight o'clock that evening, Andy demanded some Noludar,[16] a sleeping medication, and when it was delivered, he insisted that all the hostages take some. Mary drank the liquid. Although she doubted it would have any effect on her, she found herself growing weary. She closed her eyes and tried to visualize herself at home in her own bed. The night passed.

Throughout the next day, Tuesday, June 10, the negotiating team made several visits to Room 9.

Andy reiterated the demands of the inmates and requested more Demerol.

Mary began to feel their forced confinement would drag on forever. Why wasn't the government acting? Why were they allowing the inmates to hold them there for hours and hours with no respite? *Typical bureaucrats, can't ever come to any decision about anything. It's okay for them. They can sleep in a nice, warm bed. They'll wash their faces in the morning and sit down to a good breakfast. But what about us?*

Tuesday evening came, and all the hostages were allowed to make one phone call. When Mary's turn came, another hostage was brought out of the vault to take her place. She dialed our parents' home in Sechelt.

Our mother answered.

"Hi, Mom," Mary said.

"Oh, Mary," Mom replied, her voice a mournful echo. "How are you?"

"I'm fine, Mom. We're being treated okay. Everything's going to be all right, so don't worry. Just don't worry."

"Have you been given anything to eat?"

"Yeah, we had some sandwiches and pop. It's too hot to be really hungry anyway. Mom, I can't talk very long; other people are waiting to talk to their relatives, so I'd better hang up now. Take care and please don't worry."

"All right, dear, I'll try not to. We love you."

"I love you too, Mom. Bye for now."

---

16 Tradename for a sedative used for insomnia; it was replaced by newer drugs with fewer side effects and withdrawn from the Canadian market in September 1990.

She hung up the phone and returned to her place on the sofa. Andy held the knife to her throat as other hostages made their calls. She tried not to think. Everything seemed so surreal. A waking nightmare. A lump rose in her throat and she fought back tears as she thought of how our mother had sounded, and how much she must be worrying. *Oh, stop it!* she admonished herself. *Stop being a baby! Everything will be okay.*

After all the hostages made their phone calls and returned to the vault, Bruce relaxed a bit and began to move around in Room 9, talking in a low voice to Lucas. Mary lay down on the sofa, pulled a small blanket over herself, and closed her eyes. Images of the past mingled with thoughts of the present. Her training at Essondale, her experiences with patients at 999 Queen Street, Matsqui and the inmates there, her time at SFU and UBC, and her first year as a social worker at the Pen.

And here I am, she thought. *A hostage. I should have stayed home yesterday, like Penny said.*

The sound of voices woke her. She opened her eyes.

Andy was trying to inject himself with more Demerol brought in by the prison officer.

"Having any trouble?" Mary asked.

"Don't talk to me," Andy retorted. "I don't want fuck all to do with you." He turned away, and Mary closed her eyes again. She tried not to let his remark bother her. But it did.

She had seen from the outset that there was little to be gained in trying to talk to Andy. Any attempt on her part to dissuade him from carrying out his plan was futile, at least at that point in the hostage-taking. Nothing short of an act of God would change his mind. She felt powerless to change things.

She checked her watch. It was 12:40 a.m. on Wednesday morning. She fell into a light, troubled sleep.

Suddenly, shouts and curses filled the room. Bolting upright from the sofa, she saw Lucas at the vault door. He was pushing against the door with one hand, trying to open it. With the other he slashed away with his butcher knife at the hostages inside who were trying to close it. Blood was pouring down his face.

Mary's heart began to pound. No time to think. Andy was on her in a minute, grabbing her around the shoulders, pushing the point of the knife against her neck.

"You've done it now, you bastards," he shouted. "I'll kill her!"

Mary could feel her strength leaving her.

Someone from inside shouted back, "We don't care; she's one of you anyway!"

The implications of the remark had no time to register. Clutching Mary close to his chest, Andy whirled her around to face the Dutch door. Pounding footsteps shook the corridor, and someone shouted, "Cool it, Andy, cool it!"

Suddenly, uniformed guards appeared at the Dutch door. To the right of the door, a window shattered.

Guns! Pointing at her!

"Don't shoot! Don't shoot!" she cried.

A burst of gunfire!

Mary felt a searing pain in her shoulder. No time to pray for help before the second bullet ripped through the delicate white skin of her chest, entered her body, and shattered in an instant her courageous heart.

She collapsed onto the floor. Her blood, red and thick, oozed through the open wounds and spilled out on the office floor.

The prison nurse rushed to her side.

Mary took one last deep, lingering breath.

And then she was gone.

12
REQUIEM

*Oh Lord,
You gave her to us
to be our joy and you have taken her away from us;
we give her back to You without a murmur,
but our hearts are
wrung with sorrow.*

—St. Ephrem of Syria

IN A FRACTION OF A second, a life can change forever.

And so it was for me in the early morning hours of June 11, when the phone rang and a female caller identifying herself as a representative of the B.C. Penitentiary asked if I was Mary Steinhauser's sister.

"Are you sitting down?" she continued.

"Yes."

"Is there someone there with you?"

"Yes," I mumbled, barely able to breathe.

And then a very long pause before she delivered the awful news. "I'm very sorry to inform you that your sister, Mary, is dead."

It was the exact moment when my life as I knew it changed forever.

Numb with shock and disbelief, I was too stunned to ask why or how she died.

Of course I'd known about the hostage-taking since the Monday morning it began. For the next forty-one hours I'd kept a vigil of sorts... listening to the news on the radio, reading any newspaper I could find, watching TV, pacing, calling my mom and dad in Sechelt, calling Penny, Mary's roommate in Vancouver.

But through it all, it never occurred to me, not once that Mary wouldn't come out alive.

The rest of that day was a blur. My weeping mother called and we talked for a few moments, but her grief was so raw that I hardly knew how to console her. She asked when my husband and I would be coming to Vancouver. I said we'd be there as soon as we could catch a flight later that day. I called my school principal and told him I wouldn't be teaching for the week and didn't know when I'd return. I ran down to the corner bank to get some money; finding it still closed, I knocked wildly on the windows and collapsed in tears in the arms of the clerk who unlocked the front door to let me in.

We quickly packed and caught the late afternoon flight to Vancouver. At the airport, we fell into the arms of my mom and dad who'd come from Sechelt to meet us.

The next five days were a tangled chaos of anguish and sadness as we went through the motions of preparing for the funeral. Choosing the church for the requiem mass, selecting a coffin, deciding who the pallbearers were going to be, selecting a cemetery, a plot, and a grave marker… All the exquisitely painful details of preparing to inter Mary, a beloved daughter and sister.

But another shock was in store for us.

Immediately after the shooting, various news outlets reported that Mary had been stabbed to death, presumably by one of the two inmates who were carrying knives at the time. However, after completing his autopsy, the pathologist revealed that Mary had not been stabbed at all; rather, she'd died of two gunshot wounds, one to the shoulder and another through the heart.[17]

How could it be? Impossible.

None of the inmate captors were in possession of any firearms, at any time, during the forty-one hours. It had to be a member or members of

---

17 Doug Jack, J.P., *Proceedings of the Inquest on the Death of Maria Elizabeth Steinhauser*, Witness Testimony, Booklet I (New Westminster, B.C.: May 26, 1976), 6–7.

the six-man armed prison tactical squad. The would-be rescuers, who'd charged the vault area, guns blazing, in their ill-fated rescue attempt gone horribly wrong.

But on this day, Monday, June 16, the day we buried Mary, all we knew or cared about was that she was gone. My parents had lost their beloved firstborn child, their eldest daughter. I had lost my big sister, my only sibling.

We knew that her funeral would be a public event, a news story played out for all the world to see, with our grief on full display. Those five days we waited from the Wednesday to the following Monday were the most difficult of all. It was the anticipation of this dreaded event, the uncertainty of how we could endure this most painful day of our lives, how we would feel listening to the eulogies, how would we walk behind her coffin, watching it being loaded into the hearse and carried away to the cemetery. How could we bear the sadness of it. Those days had a nightmarish quality.

We had to perform the rituals though and go through the motions, even though secretly in my heart of hearts I never believed for one moment that Mary was actually dead. How could she be?

She was too young, too vibrant, and too much alive!

It was a hoax, I decided. A charade. A very bad play in which we were unwilling participants.

Now we were in the front row of the Blessed Sacrament Church. To our left was the coffin. I glanced at it from time to time. It was difficult to look elsewhere. But how could we believe she was actually in that pink brocaded box, with all those flowers on top? It seemed heavy enough to be true, but then it could have been a half dozen bags of cement in there, or some other person.

But Mary? No, no…not Mary.

Why did everyone in the congregation look so mournful, so depressed? Why were they weeping, their sobs punctuating the stillness of the room? What did they know that we didn't?

Gradually my gaze fell on the group of young girls and boys grouped around the organist to the right of the altar. Their shining faces and fresh complexions contrasted so cruelly with the very idea of death. They reminded me of Mary and me when we sang in such a choir, proud of our ability to perform in French even though we understood only portions of what we were singing. They reminded me of our youth and how the future had seemed to hold so much promise, so much hope, so much happiness. And now for Mary, it was over. She was dead.

The requiem mass, the mass for the repose of the soul of the dead, began.

"Eternal rest give them, O Lord, and let perpetual light shine upon them."[18]

In offering the homily and prayers, the chaplain-general of the Canadian Penitentiary Service, J.A. Nickels of Ottawa, said that he brought the sympathy and condolences of Penitentiary Commissioner André Therrien and "of all of us at headquarters and throughout our service." He had been at Matsqui, he said, and an inmate had told him, "She was a fine person—dedicated, thoughtful, helpful, never sparing herself. And she had compassion…in a hard world, she had compassion."[19]

Further, Nickels said that Mary exemplified, in her short career in the penitentiary service, the sometimes intangible good that people do in the tapestry of their lives. He added that in the example she set, there was hope that the pendulum might swing again toward public order, decency of behaviour, and discipline, as well as respect for the lives and feelings of others and individual responsibility.

As he spoke, I wondered how Mary would have felt about the chaplain's eulogy. It struck me that she would probably prefer the words of a good, close friend, or perhaps an inmate, someone she had worked with or given her time to.

I wondered too how he, a total stranger, could speak in a meaningful way about someone he'd never met, never spoken to, never even heard about until the day she died?

Yet there was comfort in the words of this man as he mused about life.

---

18   Rev. Hugo H. Hoever, ed., *Saint Joseph Daily Missal*, (New York: Catholic Book Publishing, 1961).

19   Rev. John Nickels, Chaplain General of Headquarters, eulogy at Mary's funeral service, Blessed Sacrament Church, Vancouver, B.C., M. Franz private collection, June 16, 1975.

"But what is Life for?" he asked. "Do the good, brave, courageous have the best time? The New Testament answers that the finest Life ended on the cross. Such was the life of Mary Steinhauser, who served life faithfully and gave so much to our service."

Over five hundred people filled every corner of the church, spilling out onto the steps and lawn. Among them were several of the fourteen hostages, a scattering of ex-inmates and members of law enforcement agencies from the Lower Mainland: Mounties in scarlet, the shoulder flashes and uniforms of the penitentiary service, the B.C. Corrections Branch, provincial deputy sheriffs, and the police forces of Vancouver, New Westminster, Port Moody, Delta, and the Canadian Railway. But Mary wouldn't have liked the solemn, hushed atmosphere. I half expected her to sit up in her coffin and ask, "What's going on here? Why is everyone so quiet?"

Finally, the priest announced the Mass was over. At the signal of the funeral director, the pallbearers, all women friends, lifted the coffin and bore it down the aisle. It seemed fitting somehow that six women should have the great honour of carrying Mary's casket to the waiting hearse and on to the cemetery. It was what I felt Mary would have wanted.

The pallbearers staggered only fractionally under the weight of the coffin, and although their faces were twisted sometimes with the effort of holding back their tears, you could see they were intensely proud of the final salute they were giving Mary.

As we followed the hearse out along 12th Avenue and onto Canada Way, traffic was halted at every stoplight to allow the cortege to move along without stopping. It seemed a magnificent paradox. In her life, Mary had achieved many things, but her accomplishments were known only to her close friends and colleagues. In death, she was a kind of celebrity and the world stopped momentarily to acknowledge her passing.

In life, she was a figure of controversy, someone who drew heat because she believed in voicing her opinion no matter how inimical to conventional wisdom, but in her death, all the old antagonisms and enmities fell away. She no longer posed a threat to the administration at the penitentiary, or to those with whom she worked who disagreed with her philosophy and approach to the rehabilitation of inmates. In the public eye, Mary was the ultimate victim, the true martyr, the strong yet compassionate figure. She was the one hostage everyone agreed would survive.

We arrived at the cemetery gates, and the hearse slowly and carefully negotiated the final turn. We alighted from the limousine and made our way across the lawn to where the canopy covered the coffin. We held each other close. Just the three of us, my dad and me flanking my weeping mother. Clasping each other for strength and courage to face these final moments.

Dozens of floral arrangements and wreaths were arranged about the bier; their scent, powerful and heady drifted in and out, borne by a light breeze. It occurred to me that Mary didn't like flowers very much. They reminded her of sickness and death. As a nurse, she came to detest the smell of withering, rotting flowers, the gifts of well-meaning friends and relatives to hospital patients. It was a waste too, she said, an incredible waste of money.

Must be about $2,000 worth of flowers here, I thought. *And they'll all die within days. What a waste. She wouldn't like that very much. Better that some charity, some needy group of people would have that money spent on those.*

In a barely audible voice, the priest read the Absolution over the grave. "Deliver me, O Lord, from the everlasting death on that day of terror. When the heavens and the earth will be shaken. As you come to judge the world by fire. Lord, have mercy. Christ, have mercy. Lord, have mercy."[20]

A feeling of unspeakable horror tore through me. This is what we're all destined for! Mary is just the first to know—the first among us to meet death.

The priest sprinkled the coffin with holy water and then swung the thurible over it—the smell of incense filled the air with its sweet, smoky pungence.

"Rescue her soul, O Lord. May she rest in peace."

A few more words were spoken, and then the priest gave one final blessing and turned away. We were left then, the three of us, to say goodbye to Mary.

---

20 Hoever, *Daily Missal*, 1226.

We slowly approached the coffin and touched it. It was cold and hard. Was she really in there? I still couldn't believe it.

And then we turned to greet our friends and other mourners. They came forward. Some quickly, some cautiously. Their tears mingled with our own.

It was over. We had buried Mary.

Our lives would never be the same.

Mary's first official portrait at one year old, 1943.

Mary and our mother ~1945.

At home in Lake Cowichan, B.C., ca. 1945.

From Left: Father holding Margaret (~one year old), Mother and Mary (~ four years old).

From left: Margaret and Mary in our apple orchard
Burton, B.C., ca. 1949

Fence-sitting behind our squared-off log home with the shake roof, Burton, B.C.

Life on the farm: Mary astride our Holstein cow with me looking on. The barn and outbuildings in the background.

Updated and improved: Steinhauser home and outbuildings, ~1960.

1955 Grades 5-8 Class Picture, Burton Elementary School, Burton, BC, Teacher Mr R. A. Wayling; Back Row: Second from Left, Mary (Gr. 7); Middle Row: Fifth from Left, Margaret (Gr. 5)
Burton Elementary School was a two-room school with one room for Grades 1–4 and the other for Grades 5–8. This year was one of the few times Mary and I were in the same classroom together.

1956 Grade 8 Class Picture: École Saint-Sacrement/Blessed Sacrament School, Vancouver BC
Second from Right: Mary celebrates with classmates.

From 1955-1957 our family lived in Vancouver to be close to our father who had suffered a devastating logging accident requiring hospitalization at the Vancouver General Hospital for 6 months and intense physiotherapy for the next year and a half. During this period, we attended classes at the Ecole Saint-Sacrement School. Although English was the language of instruction, French language classes were held daily for all students from Grades 1 – 8. In addition, students were expected to participate in a school-based touring festival choir with a repertoire of songs en francais.

On the rocky shoreline of the Arrow Lakes, Margaret, Amy, and neighbour's dog, Sandy, strike a pose. It's 1961, several years after the near-drowning incident in which Mary rescued Amy.

"Were you ever at her place, laughing with the earth?"
from *Song of Mary* by Penny G.

June 1960: Grade 12 Graduating class
Nakusp Jr.-Sr. High School, Nakusp BC
Mary seated third from left.

Mary as a student nurse at
Essondale Mental Hospital, Coquitlam, B.C. ~1961

Mary graduates as a registered psychiatric nurse, 1962.

Certificate of Registration in Registered Psychiatric Nurses' Association of B.C.

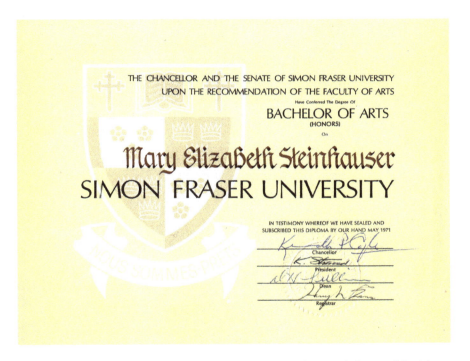

May 1971: Mary graduates with a Bachelor of Arts (Honors) in Psychology and Sociology from Simon Fraser University, Burnaby, B.C.

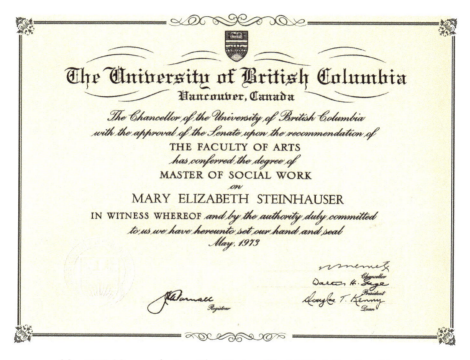

May 1973: Mary graduates with a Master of Social Work, Faculty of Arts, University of British Columbia, Vancouver, B.C.

A very proud young social worker, Mary is poised to make her mark in the world, University of British Columbia May 1973.

A bridesmaid for a friend.

Shaking hands with a pirate on a Mexican cruise.

13

1975 FARRIS COMMISSION OF INQUIRY

I REALLY WANTED TO ATTEND THE Commission of Inquiry into Events at the B.C. Penitentiary June 9 to 11, 1975,[21] which began the day we buried Mary. But it just wasn't possible. For one thing, I had to return to Toronto to finish up the school year and see my class of grade eight students graduate. Even so, I could have returned to Vancouver in early July to satisfy my overwhelming need to know how and why Mary had died so needlessly.

But a powerful instinct for self-preservation held me back. My state of mind was too fragile to withstand the trauma of listening to the details of her death. *Better to stay away,* I told myself. *You can always read about it in the papers.* So I arranged for copies of the two Vancouver dailies to be mailed to me in Toronto. Each day, as I scanned for items about the progress of the inquiry, it became increasingly apparent that some strange, inexplicable things were happening in Room 406 of the courthouse in downtown Vancouver, where the inquiry was unfolding.

In the brief opening session on Monday, June 16, Chairman Chief Justice John Farris outlined the terms of reference for the inquiry. He would be assisted by his fellow commissioners, Mr. Jack C. Lynch and Mr. Henry

---

21 Warren Allman, *Report of the Commission of Inquiry into Events at the British Columbia Penitentiary June 9 to 11, 1975.* Published by the Public Affairs Division of the Canadian Penitentiary Service and the National Parole Service (Mississauga, O.N.: Phase I Printing Ltd., released to public July 13, 1976).

F. Popp, who were all appointed by the Commissioner of Penitentiaries, André Therrien, to investigate and report on:

a. the circumstances that led to the hostage-taking;

b. the initial emergency response action;

c. the established policy and procedures prescribed at the British Columbia Penitentiary to prevent and respond to such occurrences;

d. the circumstances surrounding the detention of the hostages;

e. the measures taken to react to the situation;

f. the circumstances of the intervention of the hostages to effect their release;

g. the nature of the response reaction, which terminated the occurrence, and the circumstances in which that reaction took place; and

h. such other matters as may be relevant to this or other similar situations that might contribute to the prevention of such incidents and/or effective response and resolution of such occurrences.

Oddly enough, on this list of items no mention was made of the fact that an actual person had died in the "occurrence"; that this person, an employee of the Canadian Penitentiary Service, had lost her life while on duty in the service of her country; that this person was one Mary Steinhauser, thirty-two years old, nurse, social worker, and prison justice advocate; and that she was shot by one of her prison colleagues and bled to death on the cold hard floor of Room 9 in the Classification Building at the B.C. Penitentiary in the early morning hours of June 11, 1975.

What was even more astonishing was the failure of the authors of this document to name the woman who'd been deemed "*an example for all Canadians*" and lauded as having "*outstanding courage and fortitude in recent days*" and "*for her service in a most difficult and demanding vocation*" by the then Prime Minister of Canada, Pierre Elliot Trudeau.

Out of respect for Mary's funeral later that day, the opening session was rescheduled for Tuesday, June 17, at which time the three-man commission familiarized themselves with the physical plant at the B.C. Penitentiary. They toured the now-infamous vault area and the classification building so as to "better understand and put into perspective the evidence that will be presented to us."[22]

At around this time, a lawyer retained by the Canadian Penitentiary Service made the surprising declaration that the inquiry should not hear evidence in public on the following matters:

- The names of personnel on the tactical squad (the group that stormed the hostage vault and whose shots killed Mary)
- The number of personnel in the tactical units
- The duties of the various personnel in the tactical units under established anti-riot procedures
- The deployment of tactical squads through standing orders
- Communications systems and chains of command in the prison itself
- Standing instructions to the tactical squad and other riot personnel
- Shift changes of personnel and the prison, and the times and numbers of men
- The number of weapons and types of weapons issued to and used by prison personnel and tactical squads and anti-riot personnel
- The use of other agencies such as the RCMP, which took place from time to time in situations like this

The very first witness to testify on Wednesday, June 18, was Jim Murphy, the director of the Pacific Region of Canadian Penitentiaries. He

---
22   "No restrictions placed on B.C. Pen probe," *Vancouver Sun*, June 16, 1975, 1.

had received a call at his home on the evening of June 10 from the then solicitor-general of Canada, Warren Allmand. Allmand, he said, told him that a foreign country had been found that might accept the inmates if certain conditions were met. Allmand had ordered Murphy to discuss the information with only a limited number of specific people. This selection…was left to Murphy's discretion.

Murphy stated that Allmand told him all transportation was to be coordinated by Ottawa and that there would be no Canadian citizens accompanying inmates as hostages leaving Canada. Although Murphy had an hour to do so, he did not disclose the substance of his conversation with Allmand to the director of the penitentiary, Dragan Cernetic. Nor did he speak to any other prison official, several of whom were present in a conference room in the prison between midnight and 1:00 a.m. when the hostages made their bid for freedom.

Murphy was severely criticized by some for his failure to pass on this vital piece of information to the intermediaries, who may then have had the option of informing the inmates in tones loud enough for the hostages inside the vault to hear about this new and important development. It may have had the effect of quieting the fears of the hostages within the vault, who were by this time quietly and desperately planning their own ill-fated breakout. Abandoned by the system, so they felt, and at the mercy of the knife-wielding convicts, they were isolated and alone. Did anyone out there really care about them? Why was it taking so long for anyone to do anything?

So why did Murphy keep this information to himself? "Because it was only one more country 'considering' taking the convicts, and passing on the information would have changed nothing," he offered by way of explanation. Was this the right call for Murphy to make?

Obviously, in hindsight, it wasn't.

The second witness was Dragan Cernetic, director of the B.C. Penitentiary. Cernetic, a one-time political prisoner of the former Yugoslav government, testified that he had acceded to all the inmates' demands for drugs, candy bars, and negotiators, but he would not agree to their requests for handcuffs and leg-irons for the hostages.

"If we had issued restraining equipment, they would have had fifteen lambs on their hands. Without handcuffs," he continued, "it was possible that the hostages could act to free themselves or at least to protect themselves in the event of something going wrong."

"I ordered that the lines of communication with the convicts were to remain open at all cost," Cernetic testified. By this he meant that two unarmed prison officials, a hospital officer named Al Hadvick and Assistant Director of Prison Industries Stan Miller, were assigned to alternate in maintaining communications with the hostages through the upper half of the Dutch door. The two men were to constantly engage the inmates in conversation to find out their demands and to somehow indicate that consideration was being given to the requests.

On Thursday, June 19 and Friday, June 20, the commissioners heard the twenty-nine-page transcript of recorded messages that covered twelve of the last thirteen hours of the penitentiary siege. The transcript, submitted by Cernetic, was of meetings held in the command centre between prison officials and negotiators. A tape recording of one meeting, held at 10:47 p.m. on Tuesday evening, revealed that the hostages were "getting very anxious" and might move on their own.

Hadvick also said that "Mary for one appears to be getting a bit hysterical and started to cry and caused enough concern that I think that she might not be prepared to go along with the others (hostages) and might even put the kibosh on if something got started."

At this time, the tapes revealed the details of the proposed plan by the hostages to affect their own escape.

It was at this point that the fatal misunderstanding created by inadequate hand signals and mouthed words was laid.

"The hostages are able to get close enough to communicate with me," Hadvick revealed. "They told me that they want to make a move and I said, 'Okay fine.' I got the impression they wanted to make it right away. I said 11 o'clock, does that sound good and they said okay."

When Hadvick passed along this piece of information to the prison officials, they told him to cancel the agreement. To do so Hadvick asked that a hostage be brought out and told him that his wife was supposed to appear on television at 11:00 p.m. but that her appearance had been cancelled.

This was code for cancelling the breakout attempt. Hadvick assumed that the hostages had understood the significance of the statement.

Later events were to prove him terribly wrong.

On Monday, June 23, John Ryan, the classification officer and hostage with whom Mary had been speaking on the morning of the 9th was called to testify. He spoke of the personal terror he had undergone, largely the result of continuous frightening threats by inmate Dwight Lucas. At the time of the breakout attempt by the other hostages, John was sleeping. The first thing he remembered upon waking was someone shaking him and telling him that it was all over and that he could get up.

Ryan recounted some of the uglier, more frightening details of the hostages' confinement, such as that the three inmates were "talking about cutting a few throats and throwing a few heads out" shortly after the siege began to convince authorities that they were serious. There were also threats about "cutting a few ears and fingers and thumbs off."

He personally was constantly terrorized by Lucas, who used his razor-sharp knife to cut buttons from and shred Ryan's shirt and to cut out a pocket of his trousers. Lucas once held the knifepoint at Ryan's eye and asked him, "How would you like to lose your eyes?"

At another point, Lucas poured a bottle of antiseptic over Ryan's head until it ran down into his eyes, stinging painfully, and Lucas also kicked Ryan in the leg and groin and told Ryan he would be "the first to go" if an attempt were made to free the hostages.

Lucas also forced the hostages to take large doses of drugs that had been sent into the vault by authorities at the inmates' demand. For much of the time the hostages were the in the vault, they were forced to keep their hands on their heads, a posture that led to extreme fatigue.

At this point in the inquiry, following Ryan's testimony of the treatment he'd received as a hostage, a second hostage, corrections officer Tony Lewis, told the inquiry that he refused to testify in public. Wally Lightbody, counsel for the fourteen hostages and for several other prison employees, informed the commission that the hostages, due to concerns for their lives and safety, were categorically refusing to give evidence in public.

Farris's response was to temporarily shelve the problem by allowing Lewis to step down, with a stipulation that the commission would reassess the situation from time to time in light of evidence that they heard. It was subsequently decided, after consideration, that the hostages would give evidence in public only to those matters up until 9:00 p.m. on Tuesday evening, June 10. After that time, the hostages were prepared to give evidence fully and frankly only if it were held in camera.

On Tuesday, June 14, the hostages who were called to testify gave largely repetitious evidence about how they were confronted by three convicts with knives and had been herded into the vault, which was to be their prison for forty-one hours. But they said nothing about the crucial events just prior to their breakout attempt, the events that gave rise to the storming of the tactical squad, the events that led to Mary's death by gunshot. The hostages were then permitted by the commission counsel to complete their testimonies to limits they themselves had set.

On Wednesday, the then-security director for the B.C. Penitentiary, Fred Leech, testified that security procedures were not always followed, making it easier for inmates to try to escape. "They (the inmates) took advantage of the movement of the other inmates (the general prison population) to move to the classification building."

"It would be hard," he said, "to notice that anything was wrong in their movements at that time." Leech was reluctant to speak of the positioning of the two assault squads of six men each held near the vault. But he did say that the guards were armed with .38-calibre pistols.

It was becoming increasingly apparent to the general public, to my family, and to me that the so-called public inquiry was not public at all; in fact, all the important testimony was being heard by the three commissioners in private.

The nagging questions remained. Why was Mary the only one who'd been killed? Why had she been shot, not once, but *twice*? And why had she confided in separate conversations with her roommate Penny and with our mother that "if there ever was a hostage-taking, it would be guards who'd get me, not the inmates."

Next to provide testimony was Tom Hudson, the prison hospital officer, who had been positioned at the Dutch door at the time of the shooting.

"Bruce was positioned to the left of the vault door facing me. He was holding Mary with one arm around her. My impression was it was his left arm (holding her). Her head was slumped down. I couldn't see her face. He appeared to be holding her up. In his other arm he was holding a knife, holding it up in a raised position over Mary."

"How close?" asked the commission counsel.

"I would say within about six inches."

"Of the point of the blade?"

"Yes," Hudson said. "He shouted, 'I'll kill her!' I shouted to him, "Don't make it worse, Andy, cool it." Hudson said he shouted anything else that came to mind.

"At this time, I thought Andy was going to stab Mary," Hudson continued. "Then a window smashed to my left. Somebody shouted, 'Freeze!' and the shooting started. Everything then happened so fast. I saw Lucas go down immediately. I figured he had been shot. Almost straight after I saw blood coming from Andy Bruce's face. I saw him and Mary go down.

…

"I remember people going past me. All I wanted to do was to get over where Mary was. By this time Lucas was on his feet. There appeared to be a struggle going on. Mary and Bruce were lying sprawled out. There was lots of blood all over the place. Mary seemed to be more on her back than on her side. I'm not sure what side. I knew straight away that Mary was in critical condition in my observation of her. I didn't know where the blood was coming from. I did see a bloodstain on her chest area. I started to get her out of there into the corridor. Somebody helped me to get her out."

"Liar!" someone shouted from the public gallery when Hudson replied that he had not heard a woman shout, "Don't shoot! Don't shoot!" just before the firing began.

I wondered at what conclusions could be drawn from Hudson's statement that "Her head was slumped down. I couldn't see her face."

Either Mary had been stabbed or she'd fainted.

The autopsy performed on her body in the afternoon of June 11 by the pathologist at the Royal Columbian Hospital declared categorically that there were no stab wounds or knife injuries on her body. Clearly she hadn't been stabbed. Why then had Mary fainted? Had she fainted in those last few seconds before she was shot?

It seemed inconceivable to me. I considered the setting. After forty-one hours of confinement, of being forced to sit, to stand, to move only as allowed by Andy, there was a flurry of activity—an indication that something big was happening. Dozing or sleeping fitfully, Mary was awakened by Lucas's curses and the screams of the hostages inside the vault.

How would she react?

Certainly not by fainting in fear! Mary wasn't easily frightened or intimidated. I'd never known her to lose consciousness in her entire life.

Was she then so heavily drugged that she collapsed when Bruce forced her to act as his shield? Again, the autopsy revealed that only an insignificant amount of Noludar was present in her blood at the time of her death. Hardly enough to render a child sleepy, let alone an adult.

As the inquiry dragged on, I pondered all of these questions.

On Wednesday, July 2, after a four-day recess, the inquiry resumed. The commission heard testimony from the correctional ombudsman, Ms. Inger Hansen, who stated that the practice of solitary confinement constituted inhumane treatment. She also stated that the already volatile atmosphere in penitentiaries is aggravated by a conflict of interest between prison guards and non-security personnel, mainly because guards at the institution don't appreciate the presence of officials, whose primary goal is the rehabilitation of inmates.

Ms. Hansen told the commission that the B.C. Penitentiary guards felt they were regarded in the community as "some of the lowest people on the totem pole" because of their job. She further stated that the guards' image made them unhappy in their work, a factor that contributed to tension at the penitentiary.

On Thursday, July 3, the public and press were excluded from the inquiry. In ordering the exclusion, Chief Justice Farris was ceding to the demands of the hostages and prison guards involved, who had given notice earlier in the inquiry that they would not testify in public. The closure continued for the next five days until Thursday, July 10, when the inquiry was suddenly adjourned due to the illness of one of the commissioners.

Monday, July 21 marked the reopening of the inquiry, but again the press and the public were excluded. This time the commissioners heard testimony from the hostages and the members of the tactical squad who stormed the vault area in the final shooting.

In an article entitled, "Doubt Growing Over Secret B.C. Pen Inquiry" (in the *Vancouver Province* newspaper, Monday, July 21, 1975) Nick Hills of Southam News Service wrote:

> *The B.C. Penitentiary inquiry is clearly not giving the public the crucial facts surrounding the death of classification officer Mary Steinhauser, who was shot through the heart as guards stormed the siege area to recapture three prisoners and release their 15 hostages.*
>
> *Indeed, there is now growing doubt whether the true story concerning Miss Steinhauser's death June 11 will ever come out.*
>
> ...
>
> *Because Chief Justice Farris of the B.C. Appeal Court has been forced to take the inquiry into secret session in order to get certain evidence out of reluctant guards and prison hostages, the public's right to know all that happened in the early hours of June 11 has been substantially damaged.*
>
> *The three-man commission of inquiry may well find out, through evidence being given in camera, who fired the shot that killed Miss Steinhauser—and why. But will the public ever be told?*
>
> ...
>
> *Said inquiry counsel John Rowan: "In the interests of getting all the facts, and having balanced all the factors involved, it is my opinion that the commission should hear these witnesses in camera."*
>
> *Concurred Chief Justice Farris: "I have considered this matter too, and reached the same conclusion. I think it is*

> *in the public interest, including the safety and security of the penitentiary, that such evidence should be received in camera."*
>
> *So the inquiry has gone behind closed doors to hear exactly how and why Miss Steinhauser was fatally shot in the relief of the siege that went horribly wrong.*
>
> *For the prison staff this was the best decision—but for the general public, growing more and more alarmed about prison breakouts, hostage incidents, and treatment of prisoners, it certainly was not.*

For the remainder of the article, Hills described the doubts and rumors that were rapidly spreading throughout the community fanned by reports that Mary had screamed, "Don't shoot! Don't shoot!" as the guards stormed into the vault area; that the fatal shot had been fired from a guard's personal weapon; that no public evidence was given at the inquiry about the angle of the shot that killed her or the calibre of the bullet recovered from her body; and that although the commission itself may have acquired a clear picture of just what had happened, it was patently obvious that the public was not being given the true picture and that it was unlikely that it ever would.

> *It may be that these secret investigations, and all the secret testimony, will give the commission a true picture of what happened and why it happened. But will the general public be given the true picture after the report is sent to Ottawa?*
>
> *Certainly, there must be some doubt, after it has become clear that the so-called public inquiry set up by the Trudeau government is not public after all.*

On Wednesday, July 23, the inquiry reopened its doors to the public, but the only testimony that was heard by the commissioners referred to a new boiler system that had been installed in the penitentiary, and the fact that the institution (the B.C. Penitentiary) would be phased out by 1979.

Jim McCutcheon, the assistant director of technical services, testified that Andy had threatened to immolate the guards or the hostages if anyone approached. McCutcheon said that he had heard Andy say, "We have the stuff to turn you heroes into human torches, or we can turn these people (the hostages) into Buddhist monks."

The second witness to testify on that day was Alan Morgan, an assistant kitchen supervisor at the penitentiary, who said that a boning knife had been missing from the kitchen four days before the hostages were seized, but that he had not reported this fact to security personnel. But it was on Friday, July 25 that the most shocking headline of all appeared on the front page of the *Vancouver Sun*.

MARY'S SLAYER 'WILL REMAIN A MYSTERY FOREVER'[23]

The article began *"The identity of the man who shot and killed pen worker Mary Steinhauser will 'remain a mystery forever' according to Chief Justice Farris."* Incredulous, I read on:

> *Evidence given by two New Westminster police officers Detective Robert Rutherford and Constable Leo Braniff, the chief investigating officer and identification officer assigned to the case on June 11, had disclosed the following facts:*

1. *The bullet that had penetrated Mary's heart was fired from a penitentiary revolver—a five chamber .38 calibre revolver with a 4-inch barrel bearing the serial number D643085 and prison designation 18-A.*

2. *The shot that had struck Mary in the heart, a lead alloy bullet, was listed as coming from Revolver 18-A, and the bullet that had hit Bruce in the chin had "possibly" and "very probably" come from the same gun.*

---

23 Larry Still, "Mary's slayer 'will remain a mystery forever,'" *Vancouver Sun*, July 25, 1975, front page.

3. *The guns used had <u>not</u> been issued to the tactical squad guards by name and <u>no</u> record existed showing precisely which guard had fired what gun.*

4. *The gun from which the fatal bullet had issued was distinguishable from each of the other five guns because it had a lanyard ring on the grip of the weapon.*

5. *Members of the six man tactical squad had been sitting in a darkened room on alert, and the six guns were on the table in front of them. The men had said that when the alarm came, they simply grabbed a gun and ran.*

6. *After the shooting, five of the six guns were returned to the same room, Room 202, unloaded and the live cartridges were emptied into an ashtray on the table. It was three hours later that the five guns were turned over to Constable Braniff.*

7. *The sixth gun was given to Constable Braniff by Security Director Fred Leech on July 23, nearly six weeks later.*

How was it possible, I asked myself, that the guard possessing the gun with the lanyard ring on the butt, the gun that fired the fatal bullet, would *not* know that he held that gun? Why had it taken three hours for the five guns to be turned over to Constable Braniff, the identification officer in charge of the collection and preservation of evidence? Why had it taken nearly six weeks for the sixth gun to be turned over to the New Westminster Police Department?

But there was an explanation, Fred Leech protested when questioned outside the hearing. He was the Pen's security director, and he said that the delay in turning over the five .38s was "caused by what the men involved (the tactical squad members) had considered to be a necessity to prepare internal service reports on what had occurred. The delay in turning over the sixth gun could be explained," he said, "by the simple fact that it had been returned to the penitentiary armory through some oversight."[24]

---

24   Still, "Mary's slayer."

But the members of the tactical squad were well aware that two people had been seriously injured in the shooting and that their guns would be the most vital material evidence. And why hadn't the identification officer demanded that the guns be produced the moment he began his investigations? What conclusions could be drawn from such apparent ineptness, such blatant bungling?

The answer was quick in coming. The following day, Saturday, July 26, the headlines in the *Province* newspaper read, "Deliberate Pen coverup charged."[25] In a stunning counterpoint to his former decision to permit all the hostages and the members of the tactical squad to testify in-camera only, Chief Justice Farris named Senior Security Officer Albert Hollinger as responsible for a deliberate cover-up of evidence. Given that Hollinger had been employed by the penitentiary service for ten years and by the Montreal Police Department for five years previously, and was trained on what to do in situations like this, Justice Farris charged that Hollinger had "intentionally failed to make a record of which gun was used by which guard in the June 11 guard's assault."

Farris categorically rejected Hollinger's explanation that it was necessary to gather up the guns as quickly as possible from the siege area to ensure that none of the inmates could "get hold of one." In their final report to Parliament, the commissioners describe why they rejected Hollinger's explanation.

> *After the shooting, a member of the tactical squad, with others, entered Room 9 and assisted in getting the hostages out. He then went into the vault and saw Wilson was tied. Bruce, at this time, was on the floor bleeding profusely. Lucas, according to this officer's evidence, was standing up against the wall. Other evidence indicates that, at this time, he was handcuffed. In any event, he was surrounded by several of the prison personnel.*
>
> - *The Officer stated that he saw firearms sticking out*

---

25   Alex Young, "Deliberate Pen coverup charged," *Province,* July 26, 1975.

of the pockets of the various members of the tactical squad and "I figured if one of those guys grabbed those guns, we are in trouble."

He says that he took everybody's gun except one of the officer's gun, and took them down the hall to Room 202, where he unloaded them and put expended shell cases and live rounds in an ashtray. He kept no record of the persons from whom he obtained each particular gun. The consequence of his action was that it is now impossible to determine which person held the gun that fired the fatal shot. It is inconceivable that a man of his experience and background would not know the importance of preserving evidence and of keeping a record of the number on the gun and the person from whom he received it.

In reviewing the officer's action, it is of importance to realize that either he, or the officer with him, must have fired the fatal shot. The ballistics expert from the RCMP testified that the fatal bullet was fired from a four-inch .38 Smith and Wesson numbered D643085. This weapon is shown in Exhibit 81, and it has a lanyard ring on its butt. This weapon also probably fired the shot that struck Bruce in the jaw. There were only two persons who fired two shots or more. The remaining members of the tactical squad either fired no shots or only one. This being so, the fatal shot must have been fired by either of these two officers.

It is the opinion of the Commission that the reasonable inference is that this officer was under the impression that he had fired the fatal shot. If he had thought that it was the other officer with him, it is most unlikely that he would have mixed up the guns intentionally with the result that suspicion would be directed to him when such suspicion would be unjustified.

> *On all of the evidence, there is no doubt in the view of the Commission that this Officer intentionally mixed up the guns for the purpose of preventing it being known who fired the fatal shot.*[26]

In essence, Hollinger had tampered with material evidence to the extent that it was impossible for any investigator to determine who had shot and killed Mary. And yet, no Canadian law enforcement agency ever took it upon itself to charge Hollinger with a criminal offense, be it tampering with evidence, obstruction of justice, or any related charge. A single individual was allowed to meddle with crucial evidence, and in so doing obscure the truth forever, without so much as a slap on the hand.

The fact that Hollinger's interference with justice was publicly announced by a chief justice of the B.C. Supreme Court, and duly reported by most of the major newspapers in Canada, makes it difficult to understand how he could have escaped some kind of criminal charge or punishment by responsible public authorities.

Albert Hollinger may or may not have fired the shot that killed Mary. But it was obvious that he himself, as the commissioner pointed out, believed that he had. For what other reason would he have tampered with crucial evidence? And yet even if Hollinger admitted in the course of the inquiry that he fired the fatal shot, it's likely that he would be exonerated of blame since he was acting under orders and in the line of duty.

Why then did he try so desperately to conceal the identities of the guards who carried the weapons? Was it because in the heat of the moment, he lost his composure? Was it because he had deliberately pointed the gun in the direction of Mary and pulled the trigger, intending to "get her out of the way" so that he could get a clearer shot at Bruce? With what intent did he fire those three shots, and at whom did he aim his weapon on those three occasions?

Clearly, the answers to these questions were not forthcoming from the deliberations of the Farris Commission of Inquiry. Although the chief justice had publicly charged that a cover-up occurred within the walls of the penitentiary, he wasn't prepared to pursue the matter any further.

---

26 *Report of the Commission of Inquiry*, 36–37.

Nor did he recommend that a further exhaustive police inquiry be held to determine who fired the fatal shot.

How, then, was justice being served? I felt, deeply and bitterly, that Mary had been betrayed by the judicial system, by government and police authorities, and by society as a whole.

If her death were allowed to pass unpunished, when it was so obvious there were blameworthy elements, then it was possible that future deaths within the penitentiary system would be treated with similar leniency. What confidence could I or any other member of Canadian society have in the vigilance and sagacity of the Canadian judicial system?

Journalists in the local and national media were quick to denounce the finding of the inquiry with headlines such as, "Identity of slayer to remain 'a mystery'" (*Vancouver Sun*, July 25, 1975), "Mystery surrounds fatal bullet" (James Spears and Alex Young, *Province*, July 25, 1975), "Pen inquiry: public's right to know" (editorial, *Province*, July 25, 1975); "Deliberate Pen coverup charged: Security chief named by Farris" (Alex Young, *Province*, July 26, 1975), and "Questions unanswered as B.C. prison inquiry winds up its hearings" (Malcolm Gray, *Globe and Mail*, July 29, 1975).

Journalists raised questions about the lack of transparency; the secret hearings to hear testimony of all the hostages, most of the prison guards, and some of the penitentiary administration; and the failure of the commission to hold penitentiary officials to account for their actions or inactions.

In a scathing indictment of the entire prison system in Canada, one editorial, "Indicating a lax system" (*Globe and Mail*, July 30, 1975), lists the shortcomings of the B.C. Penitentiary, the Royal Commission of Inquiry, and the Solicitor-General of Canada, Warren Allmand, and his department. It emphasizes the failure of the system to properly examine and tell the truth about how and why Mary died. The list includes the lax security in the prison, a warden whose directives to improve security is ignored, missing prison kitchen knives not always reported missing, dangerous inmates not kept under surveillance, and a steel vault not secured and permanently sealed even though previously used to hold hostages. Another huge red flag was the refusal to discuss the tactical unit, which was made up of prison correctional officers. What training did the members have, what experience, what skill with firearms, or what emotional stability?

The editorial concludes:

Prison mismanagement is an ongoing scandal and until sufficient attention is paid to it by Cabinet and sufficient funds are made available, and until there is a Solicitor General who will make his weight felt in every prison in Canada, it will continue to be an ongoing scandal.

And thus the seeds for the B.C. coroner's inquest to occur the next year were firmly planted in the wake of a public inquiry that failed to deliver on its promises.

A woman had died and still, no one was held responsible.

The focus of the inquest would be on how and why Mary had been killed. This one, I hoped, would shed more light on all the questions that hadn't been asked or answered in the first.

It would begin the following spring in Vancouver and I would be there.

14
1976 CORONER'S INQUEST

What did Mary mean when she said,
"If there ever were any trouble at the Pen,
it would be the guards that would get me, not the inmates"?

—B.C. Chief Coroner D. Jack

"The hate in the Pen.
There was so much hate, she said."

—P.G., Mary's friend

IT WAS THE MORNING OF June 24, 1976, and I was anxiously awaiting the opening of the proceedings in the small courtroom behind the Royal Columbian Hospital in New Westminster, B.C. Here, the inquest into the death of Mary had been in progress for almost a month.

Called by B.C.'s Chief Coroner Doug Jack, the inquest would, it was hoped, answer the many questions not addressed by the Farris Commission of Inquiry the year before, specifically how and why Mary had died in a hail of bullets that fateful night just over a year ago.

I looked around me—the thirty seats in the courtroom were filled with curious spectators and the media. Presiding over the court was the coroner, a tall distinguished-looking man with a furrowed but still handsome face. To his right, the court recorder was positioned ready to key in the utterances of each witness as they delivered their all-important testimony.

Seated to the right at the front of the room was the seven-man jury, and the lawyers representing the penitentiary personnel and the inmate hostage-takers. Beside me was my good and constant friend, Sharon, who from day one had attended almost every session with me.

Today would be a day unlike any other.

Today we would finally hear from two witnesses who had never testified publicly before. The first was Penny G., Mary's close friend and roommate The second was Andy Bruce, the leader of the inmate hostage-takers, who would deliver his testimony from inside the B.C. Penitentiary, where the entire court would reconvene after lunch.

As I waited for the proceedings to begin, my mind wandered back to how I came to be in this place. It all began six months ago on a late winter afternoon of January 26. I was teaching a co-ed class of Grade 8 students at Saint Nicholas of Bari, an inner-city Toronto school, and was on my way home from work. At the subway station, I stopped to pick up a copy of the *Toronto Star* newspaper. Flipping through the pages, the headline "Steinhauser: Was she killed by B.C.s jail system?" [27] caught my eye, but it was the photo under the headline that brought me up short.

It was a picture of Mary and Andy Bruce, standing side by side, his arm around her shoulders. The caption read: *At a party in the British Columbia Penitentiary, social worker Mary Steinhauser 32, posed with Andy Bruce, a prisoner, two weeks before she was killed.*[28]

I'd never seen this picture before.

Who released this photo to the media and why? Was it an innocent homage to the close relationship Mary had fostered with an inmate she believed was capable of reclaiming his life?

Or was there something more sinister at foot?

In the weeks and months after Mary was killed, slanderous rumours and innuendos had begun to emerge about the nature of the relationship between Mary and Andy Bruce. One film producer, hoping to make a movie of the hostage-taking, publicly made the dubious supposition

---

27 Timson, "Steinhauser." A6.
28 Ibid.

that Mary had been a victim of Stockholm Syndrome[29]; a TV journalist inferred in an interview with me that Mary was a naïve, starry-eyed fan member of a band of outlaws-on-the-run. "Was Mary an inmate groupie?" she asked. Or even more outrageous, the suggestion that Mary and Andy were lovers, a notion that later informed the plot of a yet-to-be-written Canadian play, *One Tiger to a Hill*. All of these questionable rumours, plus the even more egregious one that Mary had known about and was complicit in the hostage-taking itself, gave me cause to be very suspicious of what was published in the press and why.

The real story behind this photo was quite different. I recognized it as one of many pictures taken just two weeks before the hostage-taking, on Community Awareness Day at the B.C. Penitentiary. When emptying Mary's briefcase of its contents shortly after she died, I found a number of prints all taken at the same event, including one that caught my eye. It was a group picture with Andy Bruce standing side by side with another woman while Mary stood at the far side of the same group. Clearly, Mary wasn't the only woman Bruce had posed with that day.

I began to read the article below the photo.

"*There is a file folder lying in the office of New Westminster Coroner Doug Jack. The number on it is 75 ML 135, and inside is a medical certificate of death for one Mary Steinhauser, 32*" the article by *Star* staff writer Judith Timson began.

It went on to say that Mr. Jack hoped to hold an inquest into Mary's death within six weeks; at which time, Timson wrote, "*Jack expects to call Albert Hollinger, a man with 10 years' experience within the penitentiary system and another five as a Montreal policeman. Whether or not Jack will call inmate Andy Bruce, whom Jack refers to as a 'horse of a different colour,' is still up in the air,*" because of, as Timson continued, Jack's apprehension that Bruce will have "*anything concrete to say.*"

Timson continued, "*That view, and the fact that Jack definitely intends to 'avoid the element of blame' during his inquest, make it unlikely that critics of*

---

29 An emotional attachment to a captor formed by a hostage as a result of a continuous stress, and a need to cooperate for survival.

the public inquiry held last summer to investigate Steinhauser's death will be satisfied that the truth about the incident is about to come out now."[30]

At that point, I might have anticipated the eventual outcome of the inquest, but I was optimistic that justice would finally prevail. It was inconceivable to me that the person who had shot my sister and mixed up the guns would not be held accountable for his actions.[31] And how could I ignore my feelings that the federal government and the penitentiary system had closed ranks to protect and shield the guard or guards responsible for Mary's death?

If someone had died as a result of my negligence or my actions, I reasoned, wouldn't the law have done its utmost to bring me to justice? Why was it different for Mary? Wasn't she entitled to the same treatment as any other citizen of a democratic, law-abiding country?

Even though I didn't know it at the time, there was one more critically important reason to be at the inquest, which was only revealed to me in July 1976.

In the eighty-three page *Report of the Commission of Inquiry into Events at the British Columbia Penitentiary June 9 to 11, 1975*, there was **not one mention of Mary Steinhauser** as the sole hostage killed on June 11, 1975. Rather, in dozens of references, Mary is referred to as "the hostage," "the Classification Officer," "the officer," "the first hostage," "the hostage in Room 9," "the hostage killed during the incident," or "the hostage killed during the hostage-taking."

Mary Steinhauser had ceased to exist. No trace of her was to be found.

Incredulous, I asked myself: *How is it possible that, in the entire report, Mary's name was not mentioned? Not once.*

How could it be that this document, the *Report of the Commission of Inquiry into Events at the British Columbia Penitentiary June 9 to 11, 1975*, an official federal government report, published by the Public Affairs Division of the Canadian Penitentiary Service and the National Parole

---

30 Ibid.

31 Larry Still, "Inmate names guard in Steinhauser death," *Vancouver Sun*, January 21, 1976, front page.

Service, under the authority of then-Solicitor General of Canada Warren Allmand *would NOT name* the person, the Canadian peace officer in the employ of the federal government, a respected social worker and outstandingly brave and committed advocate for inmates, who had given her life to shield and protect not only her colleagues but the inmates themselves?

On the first day of the inquest, I learned that there would be twenty-nine witnesses in all, twenty-seven men and one women, who would be called to testify over the next six weeks. These witnesses included police personnel, penitentiary and medical personnel, hostages, inmate hostage-takers, and members of the prison tactical squad. Finally, later in the inquest, Penny, Mary's friend and roommate, would also be called to testify.

Also in attendance and permitted to question the witnesses were lawyers representing the penitentiary staff and the two inmates. As Mary's sister, I too, was granted permission to ask questions of all the witnesses.

Declaring the proceedings open, the coroner stated that the inquest was not a trial, but a fact-finding commission based on sworn evidence and was not intended to judge the guilt or innocence of anyone.

Over the first month of the inquest, there were ten days of testimony in which police and penitentiary personnel reported on the physical details of Mary's death, the political and administrative responses to the hostage-taking, the penitentiary layout, how she died, and the chaos and confusion of the ensuing aftermath. One by one, the witnesses gave often shockingly graphic descriptions of the wounds Mary suffered, of the final moments when she breathed her last, and the blood, oh, the blood…that spilled out over the floor of Room 9 in those final seconds of her life.

Each testimony was painful to endure, but I forced myself to listen, to take notes, to blot out the still open and raw wounds of my heart. I forced myself to close off my emotions so I could listen and record.

But where was Mary in all this? I wondered. *Where was her essence, her humanity, her passion, her bravery?*

It all seemed so cold, so clinical, so inhuman.

Finally, on Day 11, the court would hear from two witnesses who knew Mary well and had spent time with her in the hours and days leading up to the hostage-taking. These were Penny G. and Andy Bruce himself.

I agonized over the moment when I would face Andy Bruce for the first time. Could I hold myself together long enough to utter the few urgent questions I had for him? Or would my voice fail me at this most important time in my life?

Penny was the first to appear. She'd been hastily subpoenaed in the early weeks of the inquest to clarify the disturbing comment Mary made to her at some point shortly before her death, which Penny subsequently repeated to me. Describing this comment as a kind of dying declaration, the coroner was determined to find out what Penny knew about Mary's provocative and incriminatory comment.

I whispered a silent plea that a reluctant Penny would find the courage to speak about this comment, about the days and months leading up to June 9, and about Mary's attitude toward work, her working conditions at the penitentiary, and her hopes and fears for her future, both personal and professional.

The coroner began.[32]

What did Mary mean when she said, "If there ever were any trouble at the Pen, it would be guards who would get me, not the inmates"?

Penny explained that it was during one of many such conversations in which "Mary talked about her work all the time—like, every night, you know. She was very involved in what she was doing."

What was the tone of the remark, the coroner asked. "Was it said in a rather serious tone, do you feel, or was it said in a rather jocular, off-handed fashion?"

"I would say sarcastic," Penny replied.

Later on in the proceedings, one of the lawyers asked Penny to describe her interpretation of Mary's remark. She replied, "…well, like I say, I wasn't surprised that she said that. I got the impression that Mary didn't have the highest opinion in the world of the guards' capabilities, you know."

---

32 The following witness testimonies (including transcription dialogue) to the end of this chapter are from the *Proceedings of the Inquest on the Death of Maria Elizabeth Steinhauser*, Booklet XI, 2–24.

The coroner continued his questioning about what Penny knew about Mary's work at the penitentiary.

There was such hostility in the penitentiary. "The hate in the pen. There was so much hate she [Mary] said." In spite of the prevailing culture of hate within the prison environment, however, mainly between the guards and the inmates, Mary had a keen interest in working on penal reform; she was very enthusiastic about her work with the taskforce in Ottawa. She had a strong desire to effect change in the system, Penny continued. "She was dynamic."

Continuing on with his questioning about Mary's forebodings of an imminent hostage-taking or prison breakout, the coroner asked, "Was there any evidence that you could perceive that she [Mary] was apparently much more upset then [sic] she had been say a week or two or a month or so beforehand? Did she impart anything to you that she was afraid of any occurrence that was going to happen?"

"Well she didn't say that she was afraid of any occurrence but she did say—it was on the Friday before the incident on the Monday—she said that she had seen Andy Bruce and that when he got up to go he said, 'What if I refuse to go?' and sort of stood there and—"

"She told you this?" the coroner queried.

Penny confirmed that she did, and further that Mary replied to Andy, "'Well, there's nothing much I can do about it, I guess.' Like, she was at her desk and he was going, like, leaving and then he went. She was talking about that that weekend to the extent that I suggested to her that she not go into work on Monday. I said, 'Why don't you just not go into work on Monday,' but…"

The coroner continued his questioning. "What made you suggest that perhaps she [Mary] shouldn't go in, shouldn't have gone to work on the following Monday?"

Penny replied that she felt Mary was upset, that she was afraid. But Mary, being Mary—absolutely dedicated to her work—simply ignored Penny's plea.

How did Mary feel about Andy Bruce? What was the nature of her interest in him specifically? the coroner queried. "Let's put it this way, did she appear to be interested in Andy Bruce as opposed to any other inmate of the penitentiary?"

"Uh, I wouldn't say she was vitally interested in him in that sense but—I don't know why she mentioned his name. Well, possibly because of this social that she had to put on for this—the annual social, and that he had helped her quite a bit in collecting the money from the prisoners and stuff like that, and his name did come up and she felt that he was a dynamic person, and that he was a leader and that he could possibly help other native inmates within the prison system."

"So now you're expanding on her thoughts in the matter. She obviously told you a lot more then [sic] you've already said, that he was a dynamic person and all the rest of it."

"Yeah," Penny said. "She felt that about him that he could be a leader, you know."

The next questioner, one of the lawyers for the inmates, returned to the issue of the climate of hate in the penitentiary that Mary referred to and the possibility that the guards were hostile to her. Here is the transcript of that conversation.

> LAWYER #1: Were there other discussions about the hate and so on in the penitentiary that you've had with her [Mary]?
>
> PENNY: Conflict, yes, uh huh.
>
> LAWYER#1: What sort of conflict?
>
> CORONER: And I take it that she had mentioned this dissatisfaction before?
>
> PENNY: Yes, well, she had, from what I could gather, treated the inmates that she saw like human beings instead of like possibly how the guards might treat them, you know.
>
> LAWYER #1: Did she feel, in the penitentiary, that because of the hate that was so all-permeating that it was difficult for someone who get reform for the prisoners to work there?

CORONER: Do you understand that?

PENNY: I understand that it was practically impossible to put into effect any reforms in the penitentiary. That was the impression I got. It was extremely difficult.

LAWYER#1: Did she talk about why it was so difficult to reform things?

PENNY: Uh, she did talk about why it was so difficult to reform things, for hour after hour, but they were general things. They were things that she was frustrated about and that's why when something like the task force came up she was so enthusiastic. There was something, at least, that she could do.

LAWYER #1: Was this task force working on segregation? Was that part of its—

CORONER: Do you know this? Did she mention to you—

PENNY: No, all I know is that it's something to do with the amalgamation of the Canadian Penitentiary Service and the National Parole Board and she had her literature there but I never read it. In fact, I leafed through it and that's not my thing, you know.

LAWYER #1: Now, you said that she didn't have the highest opinion of some of the guards or the guards. Can you tell us whether she said that the guards didn't have a high opinion of her as well? Did she talk about that kind of conflict?

PENNY: No.

At this point, Lawyer #1 turned to the subject of the Community Awareness Day. After establishing that Penny had not attended that event, he then asked her what she knew about Mary's work on the "social" as Penny described the Community Awareness Day.

LAWYER #1: Was it your impression from talking with Mary that that was something she worked on quite hard, quite a lot?

PENNY: That social that she had you mean?

LAWYER #1: Yes.

PENNY: Oh yeah, she talked about that for weeks, you know organizing everything and organizing the entertainment and getting them cleared and money and invitations. Yeah, she was really involved in it.

…

CORONER: If I may, at this point, Miss G., after it was over and done with, was she quite pleased with the project as being a success?

PENNY: Yes, she said it went off very well.

…

In the final minutes of her testimony, the coroner invited me, as Mary's sister, to question Penny. He referred to me throughout the inquest as Mrs. Haronitis (my married name at the time).

MRS. HARONITIS: Did Mary ever talk about the attitude of the penitentiary officials and some of the guards towards women in the penitentiary system?

PENNY: Uh, chauvinistic.

CORONER: Did she actually say that?

PENNY: Oh yeah.

CORONER: To whom was she referring?

PENNY: Well, I have to be fair because she actually said that the prisoners were chauvinistic too.

CORONER: The prisoners were chauvinistic as well as who?

PENNY: As the guards, well, the prison officials.

> CORONER: Did she specifically state guards as opposed to officials. The word official carries a wide spectrum [sic].

> PENNY: I can't remember. I don't know who the officials were—the guards and the prisoners.

> ...

The coroner asked Penny one final question.
CORONER: Miss G., you rather smiled when the subject of chauvinism raised its ugly head. What caused you to smile? Was this kind of a jocular, at least a laughable point as far as you and Mary were concerned, being both of the feminine gender?

> PENNY: Well, Mary was very dynamic and she didn't like sort of being restricted because she was very intelligent and dynamic.

> After posing a few more points of clarification, the coroner thanked Penny and indicated she was excused. Her testimony was over.

Later on that afternoon, the inquest moved to the B.C. Penitentiary to hear the explosive testimony of the inmate hostage-taker, Andrew Bruce.

15
INMATE HOSTAGE-TAKER

ANDREW BRUCE testifies[33]

SINCE THE DAY I FIRST learned Mary was taken hostage by three desperate prison inmates led by one Andrew (Andy) Bruce, the mastermind of the trio, I was filled with fear and loathing for this man.

It was Andy who held a butcher knife with a fourteen-inch blade to Mary's throat throughout the forty-one hours, whenever there was any communication between himself and the prison personnel or negotiators.

It was Andy who used Mary as a human shield to protect himself from harm in those final horrific seconds of the ill-fated, blood-soaked rescue attempt.

It was Andy who exposed Mary, his advocate, his friend, and his trusted counsellor, to such danger that she paid with her life for her kindness and trust in him.

It hardly mattered to me that a guard's bullet had been the actual cause of Mary's death; I still felt that the onus for her death should rest squarely on Andy Bruce's shoulders.

Yet, as I learned from Penny after Mary died, Mary had liked this man. She'd seen something in Andy, felt he was capable of redeeming himself and could, if given the chance, begin a new and better life after he'd served his time. She had spent so much time working with him, essentially

---

33 Andrew Bruce's witness testimony taken from the *Proceedings of the Inquest on the Death of Maria Elizabeth Steinhauser*, Booklet XI, 37–164.

befriending him, counselling him, and offering him hope that he could eventually rise to take his place as a leader in his community.

I also wanted to know what Andy would say about his motives for the ill-fated escape attempt. Why did he, Dwight Lucas, and Claire Wilson make such a bold, reckless, and seemingly impossible attempt to escape from the fortress-like penitentiary by the taking of hostages? What was their motivation for such a radical plan? This afternoon we would hear from him.

When Andy finally appeared in the courtroom that afternoon, handcuffed and shackled at the ankles and clothed in green prison garb, I studied him carefully. I wanted to get the measure of this person who'd cost my sister her life and our family so much pain and anguish.

So defiant, so young, yet so vulnerable he seemed.

Unbidden and unexpected, a wave of something resembling compassion washed over me at the sight of this young man, chained, bound, unable to walk or move freely.

Why did he, Dwight Lucas, and Claire Wilson hatch such an ill-fated plan? What were their motives?

The coroner began his questioning.

As Andy recounted it, his prime motive for planning the hostage-taking was his strong belief that he was being marked by the guards to be returned to the solitary confinement unit, that he was getting a lot of "heat" from the prison guards, that they'd soon be making the "grab"—that is, taking him back to solitary, the hateful, dreaded place he'd been to before once in 1971 and again in 1972. He was reminded of this when hearing reports from both Dwight and Claire that, in the days before, they'd been frisked and questioned by the guards when they returned from visiting him in his cell. "They're going to grab you. They're going to take you from population,"[34] some inmates said.

Recounting how galling it was to learn of this, Andy testified at how unjust it was and how angry he felt. He'd been keeping out of trouble. In the six months since he was back in the population, he'd held two responsible, elected positions in the penitentiary, one as the secretary of the

---

34 The group of inmates in the prison who had the freedom to move around to associate with others and work at a particular job.

Community Awareness Group and the other as the president of the Native Brotherhood. Not only that, but he'd also been involved in a drug study.

Because Mary was the liaison for the Community Awareness Group, Andy had frequent contact with her, and she clearly felt he was doing a very good job with all the preparations and planning for the banquet. But, in spite of the fact he was doing all the things he was supposed to do, Andy was still being threatened with further confinement, with being returned to that hated place, the "Penthouse", as it was known.

Nor was there any recourse or appeal process for the inmate. Appealing to his own classification officer or to Mary would be fruitless, he said, because neither could intervene on a matter of prison security. There was no one he could talk to at that time.

Feeling there was nothing to lose, he, Lucas, and Wilson began to talk about giving the guards a "reason to put us up there," and set their plan in motion.

Over the weekend, the three reclaimed various knives they had secreted in hiding places around the prison, and secured some blank passes to have on hand to allay any suspicions the guards might have about their movements around the Pen the following Monday.[35]

That morning, the three inmates led by Andy, each bearing a knife, burst into the classification building, quickly taking the guard on duty at knifepoint, rounding up all the other classification officers, and herding them down to the vault.[36]

It was in this vault that the twelve male and two female hostages were kept for the next day and a half. Isolating the hostages in this way was Andy's plan; he felt it would wear down their defenses and keep them in line. He and Dwight also devised a "good cop, bad cop routine," in which

---

35 Permission notes from penitentiary staff gave inmates the right to move around the prison on specific errands or tasks.

36 At about the centre of the outside wall of Room 9 is a small windowless room approximately 11 feet, 9 inches deep and 16 feet, 2 inches wide. In the vault are two rows of shelves in the centre portion and shelves on the two side walls, which are made of concrete. There are ventilation holes only, no windows. Entry to the vault is through two doors. The first door is a swinging door that swings in an arc from right to left. Immediately behind this is a steel sliding door without stops at either end. The result is that the door can be pulled so as to leave a space at either end.

Andy was the "good cop" and Dwight Lucas the "bad cop," wherein Andy would make concessions and show some kindness to the hostages while Lucas terrorized them.

I shivered, recalling John Ryan's previous testimony.

But Mary, as Andy described, was sometimes by herself in Room 9 while he and the two other inmates were inside the vault with the fourteen other hostages.

The coroner asked about this. "Did you, at any time, say, 'Okay, take off. We're going to do something drastic'?"

Andy replied, "No, no. I didn't tell her that we were going to do anything drastic. I kept her outside the vault, like I said, because I knew what was going to come down inside, the kind of atmosphere that was going to be created. I had her out there because I knew her from previous conversations in meetings that I had had with her. I knew how she would react to me, right. Specifically, I knew that she was completely nonviolent and in a situation like that if she had been thrown a weapon or anything, she would have dropped it rather then [sic] use it, you know. So that was part of the reason why I had her out there."

The coroner asked Andy to clarify. "In other words, you had much more faith in her then you had in the rest of them?"

"Yeah," Andy replied. He also mentioned he'd asked Mary on a few occasions if she wanted to go, if she wanted to leave, and she had declined.

But why? I wondered… Why hadn't Mary left Room 9 to save herself?

> MARGARET: Now, if, in fact, you had establish [sic] a rapport as you have stated with Mary, you obviously had some respect for her as a person. What reason can you provide for the fact that you did subject her personally to a gruelling forty-one hour endurance test that eventually resulted in her death?

> ANDY: Like I said, what she underwent—she had been offered, on different occasions—I didn't subject her to the forty-one hour period. I asked her on different occasions if she wanted to leave. She could have left any time she wanted to. The reason I had her out front with me, like, out of the vault, was like I said, I knew what was going on in that vault and the conditions that were going to be created in order to keep them people in line. Like, there were twelve men and

there were three of us and the circumstance that had to be created in order to keep them in line—I just didn't want her to be a part of that.

MARGARET: Why didn't you leave her out of the entire plan? Why would you take her down to Room 9 in the first place?

ANDY: I asked her—just at that time, at the time it happened, I told her, like, when she passed me, I said, 'get down to Room 9' and she went down there, right. Now, when I first offered for her to leave was shortly after we had let Innes,[37] right, Innes go.

When the coroner interrupted to enquire if Innes was the man with the heart condition, Andy replied, "Yeah, we had told him that he could leave and I asked her shortly after that, 'Do you want to go. Do you want to leave?' You know. She said, 'No, I'll stay here.' She more or less implicated to me that she wanted to stay with them people that were in the vault, her friends that were in the vault. She wanted to be around them."

So Mary stayed.

Nor did she try to convince Andy that the hostage-taking was a futile act. Conversely, neither did she encourage him to carry on with what he was doing.

"There was very little conversation about it, as a matter of fact," Andy testified. "When she started asking questions about it, you know, I just said, 'I ain't going to talk about this. This is what its [sic] come to, right. This is it. I got no other alternative.'" As an aside, he reiterated that there was nobody he could turn to, nobody who could alleviate what was coming down on him, and that the guards were perpetrating the actions in the first place.

As the hours wore on, the inmates demanded injectable drugs, specifically Librium, Noludar, and Demerol,[38] be brought into Room 9, mainly

---

37 The guard who was released by the inmates because he had a heart condition.

38 Chlorodiazepoxide, trade name Librium, is a sedative and hypnotic medication used to treat anxiety, insomnia, and withdrawal symptoms from alcohol and/or drug abuse. Methyprylon, trade name Noludar, was a sedative used for treating insomnia, but is now rarely used as it has been replaced by newer drugs with fewer side effects. Pethedine, also known as Demerol, is a synthetic/opioid pain medication similar to morphine.

to keep themselves calm. But Andy was suspicious that the drugs may not be what they were purported to be, so he demanded that a certain drug he assumed was Demerol should be tested on one of the hostages before taking it himself. Mary offered herself as the guinea pig, so Andy injected Mary with 10 ccs of Demerol. When Mary appeared to have no adverse reaction to the injection, he then gave himself a shot of the drug.

As the day wore on, time was hanging heavy on their hands. Andy, who'd just learned how to operate the VTR (video tape recording) machine, began filming the hostages.

"I was filming the hostages. I filmed Hadvik and Miller at the door.[39] You know, I was filming the hostages and I was asking them if they had anything to say, if they wanted to say anything into the audio part of the camera. Several of them did say things, you know. There were things they were saying in regards to their being held hostage and the way they felt and, in particular, Mary made a statement about well—it was actually an analogy between them and the Cross–Laporte thing with the FLQ[40] last year that their lives—like if we were ministers they wouldn't be in that situation. They wouldn't have had to be in that situation for the amount of time that they were."

At around 12:30 in the morning on the second night of the hostage-taking, everything appeared to be calm inside the vault. The door was open about eight to ten inches. Outside in Room 9, where Mary was sleeping on the sofa, Dwight was asleep on a chair with his back to the vault door, and Andy was sitting on a chair beside the table watching TV.

Suddenly, out of the corner of his eye, Andy saw the vault door slowly shutting. He jumped out of his chair, over the couch, and grabbed the

---

39 Hadvik was the penitentiary health care officer; Miller a penitentiary official.

40 The 1970 kidnapping and subsequent murder of Pierre Laporte, Minister of Labour and Deputy Prime Minister in the Liberal Government in Quebec, Canada, by members of a separatist group, the Front de Libération du Quebec or FLQ as they were commonly referred to. Also kidnapped around the same time was James Cross, a British diplomat, who was held in captivity for sixty-two days until he was released by the hostage-takers in exchange for a flight to safety in Cuba. Though exiled from Canada for life, the hostage-takers were allowed to return in the late 1970s to serve their sentences in a Canadian prison.

top of the door, all the while yelling at Dwight to get up. Together they tried to pry the door open, but only managed to stop it from closing about six inches.

Just then, one of the hostages reached through with a tripod and hit Dwight over the head twice in quick succession. Andy shouted, "Watch it!"

The hostages said, "Hit him again!" and the one with the tripod hit Dwight again.

Simultaneously Hudson, the health care officer, was at the Dutch door shouting to the people in the vault, "Cool it, open the door you guys!… Cool it, cool it. Open the door you guys."

Andy reached around with his right arm and grabbed Mary, who was now getting up from the couch, holding her in the arc of his arm while with his left hand, he pointed the blade of the knife just inches from her throat. "Open the door or I'll kill her!" he screamed at the one male hostage still visible just inside the vault.

And the hostage replied, "Go ahead, she's one of you anyway," and began screaming for help, another male hostage adding his voice to the plea.

Andy continues. "That's when everybody started screaming and yelling and I just—there was nothing I could do. I wasn't—I had no intention of killing her. I never did have any intention of killing. I just let the door go, you know. I turned around. I heard them people coming down from—I imagine they were at the trailer anyway. That's what it sounded like to me, right, was that they were coming in, running and hitting the wall and bracing themselves against the wall before they ran down the hallway. They were running down towards the Dutch door, right. I turned around. I had Mary in front of me. I said, 'I guess it's time to go home, right.'"

Suddenly, two guards with guns drawn appeared at the Dutch door. The first to appear was Hollinger and right behind him, Nelmes.[41] Unable to get a clear shot of the inmates, Hollinger moved over to the window to the right of the Dutch door, smashing the Plexiglas window. Without saying a word of warning he fired at Andy, hitting him in the chin. Moments later, Nelmes fired in the direction of Mary and Andy. That bullet, it was

---

41   Hollinger and Nelmes were members of the prison tactical squad.

later determined, was most likely the bullet that hit Mary in the shoulder, exiting her body and finally hitting Andy in the teeth. Both Mary and Andy went down.

As Andy recalled that moment:

"I got hit and we both went back and we both went down. She slumped off to her right and I was just down. I had my hands on my chin because the blood was just pouring out. I grabbed my chin and I was trying to push it like this [indicating] but it didn't do any good because the blood was still going all over the place. Like I say, she slumped over to her right and she started coming up. Like he [Hollinger] was still standing at the window when she started coming up, and she was screaming not to shoot me, right. 'Don't shoot him,' right. She was pushing herself up with—"

After further questioning, he continued.

"Now she was pushing herself up with her arm and she looked like this [indicating] at me and then she looked directly at him [Hollinger], and that's when she was hit, and when that bullet went through her she went back like this [indicating] and she hit me and then she went off to her left, right. Now I'm still down on my knees and I'm looking directly at him, and he reached through and he fired again. As this was happening, as he was firing through that door, the one window to his left—I guess it would be the window to his left and my right come out, right and it was just in my peripheral vision and there was another window behind me that smashed, right. So, before any of those people in any of them windows even shot—I didn't even hear any of them shots, just shots from that window that come directly from Hollinger's gun and hit me in the stomach. My hands come down and I grabbed it. I grabbed my stomach like this [indicating] and fell over to my left and I was behind her and, you know, I was looking at her and that's about the last thing—"

Andy finished, "The last thing I remember was that I had to move her so blood wouldn't get in her hair."

According to Dwight's earlier testimony, all the shooting took place within about ten seconds.[42] As the guards rushed in to subdue Dwight,

---

42　James Spears, "Lucas Recounts last 10 seconds of Mary's life," *Province*, Vancouver, B.C., June 23, 1976, 28.

Hudson scrambled to reach Mary. What would Hudson find? Would Mary be wounded? How badly? What would he do?

Several days would pass before we'd finally hear Hudson's eyewitness account of Mary's final seconds.

16
GO-BETWEEN

THOMAS HUDSON testifies[43]

Stationed at the Dutch door since midnight in the early morning hours of June 11, Tom Hudson, the health care officer at the B.C. Penitentiary, had an unobstructed view into Room 9 where Mary, Andrew Bruce, and Dwight Lucas were sitting. He could also see just beyond into the vault, where fourteen other classification officers had been held against their will for almost forty hours.

Hudson knew Mary; they had met on a number of occasions because her caseload included inmates who were patients in the penitentiary hospital, where he worked as a male nurse.

At approximately 12:20 a.m., Hudson overheard Andy Bruce asking Mary if she wanted any sleeping medication. She replied that because she'd slept for a long period that morning, it would be of some use to sleep, so she voluntarily drank a half cup of Noludar. Then she settled down on the settee, lit a cigarette, covered herself with the blanket, and began watching T.V. Dwight and Andy started to fix with Demerol.

A few minutes later, Hudson spoke to Mary and asked how she was, how things were. She said she'd been treated all right, and that the hostages were in reasonable condition considering the circumstances.

It looked as if it would be a quiet night.

---

43 Thomas Hudson's verbatim witness testimony taken from the *Proceedings of the Inquest on the Death of Maria Elizabeth Steinhauser*, Booklet XII, 6–27.

At this point in Hudson's testimony, the coroner interjected with "During the whole time you were on duty, Mr. Hudson, were they [the inmates] armed constantly with knives?"

Hudson replied, "Yes," and continued his testimony.

At approximately 12:50 a.m., Hudson walked down the hall to the bathroom. Suddenly, he heard a lot of screaming and shouting coming from Room 9. He raced down to the command post, paused at the door just long enough to shout, "Hit it, hit it!" then raced back down to Room 9. There was a chair just outside the Dutch door; he jumped up with one foot on the chair, and the other foot resting on the top of the lower half of the door.

"Right in front of me and slightly to the left of the vault door, Bruce was standing with his arm around Mary, his left arm, and in his right hand, he had the knife—the knife poised above her and at this time, I—I felt that Mary had been stabbed because I saw blood on Mary and she was—"

Where was Dwight Lucas?

"Lucas was standing by the vault door opening waving his knife and he shouted—I can't remember the exact words he was shouting, but he was shouting."

Did you see blood on him?

"Yes, there was—there was a fair amount of blood running down in the middle of his forehead, running down his face."

And Mary, what about Mary? I silently whispered.

She was, Hudson continued, "Slumped half forward to Bruce's left and her head was down. I couldn't see her face and I thought at this time that she had been stabbed and I shouted to Bruce, 'Cool it, Andy, cool it,' and I said some other things, which I don't recollect."

According to Hudson, Andy then shouted to him, "I'll kill her, you've done it now," and all the while, "He was facing me with Mary in front of him, one arm around her waist and the knife up, and that is very vivid in my mind. I can see it as if it was yesterday, and that was exactly the way he was standing."

Hudson recalled, "At the same instance as I was shouting to Bruce everything happened—well, as I was up on the Dutch doors, this was all in just seconds, very, very, very short space of time…"

Windows were breaking to his right and left when someone Hudson thought was Mr. Y. shouted "Freeze," and then he thought Mary was being stabbed because he saw "the knife in a downward motion."

Then the shooting started. There was "Rapid gunfire in the space of seconds. There was just a crackle of shots. I saw Bruce hit in the face and go backwards with blood gushing from his hand, down on the floor out of my sight behind the chesterfield."

And where was Mary?

"She went down with him [Andy]. They both disappeared behind the chesterfield."

After Hudson jumped over the Dutch door and undid the locks, everyone was trying to get in at the same time. Some people took Dwight away while Hudson "went round the chesterfield and saw Mary and Bruce lying in lots of blood."

Very pointedly, the coroner asked Hudson, "Incidentally, at this point or just prior to the shooting or during the shooting, did you hear Miss Steinhauser say anything?"

I held my breath as Hudson's spoke.

"Mary never said anything from that time. She never said anything, and I certainly didn't expect to hear anything because I thought that she had been injured at this time."

After an interval of several minutes of questioning, the coroner asked, "By the way, did you at any time hear Mary scream?"

"No. No, I never heard—I never heard any words. I never heard any scream from Mary at all, and this is why I was convinced at the time that I got back to those doors that Mary had been injured."

After the shooting stopped, Hudson's first action was "to get Mary out of there," because he could see she was unconscious and in critical condition. Between himself and Mr. Y., the two men carried her out into the corridor and laid her on the floor.

Hudson then said, "Initially she didn't breathe and then she gave a [he demonstrates a long sigh] long, drawn-out—"

"Gasp?" the coroner suggested.

Hudson said yes, that he was going to start external cardiac massage but, seeing blood in her chest area, felt that the thumping action would compound the damage. It was almost immediately then that the stretcher bearers arrived and carried Mary's now still and quiet body to the waiting ambulance.

17

HOSTAGE

*"The person who took my hand said not to look.
I saw blood on the wall and I just didn't look."*

—J.W., female hostage

JUROR: *Would you say she (Mary) was very compassionate?*
J.W.: *I thought she was very compassionate.*
JUROR: *Extremely so?*
J.W.: *Yes.*

Only six of the fourteen hostages who were sequestered against their will in that windowless concrete vault for forty-one hours were called to testify at the inquest. Of the six, only one was a woman.

One after the other, they recounted the terrifying, nightmarish episode on the morning of June 9, when they were rounded up like cattle to slaughter by three knife-wielding inmates, intent on breaking out of their prison fortress. As they spoke of their terror, their anguish, and their treatment at the hands of their inmate captors, I shuddered to think of how I would feel had I been one of them. I was particularly interested to hear of the experiences of two of the hostages: J.W., the other female hostage, and John Ryan, a male hostage, who had the misfortune to be the singular target and object of the most vicious treatment by Dwight Lucas.

J.W. was the first to testify.[44] As she took her seat in the witness chair, I looked at her closely. She was young—in her early to mid-twenties, I guessed—with a quiet demeanour; reserved and introspective, she was apparently uncomfortable about having to testify. Throughout her testimony, J.W. spoke as if still traumatized by the experience. She frequently noted that her memory was quite vague about many details of her experience.

She'd only been employed as a classification officer at the B.C. Penitentiary for eight months, with a caseload of about forty inmates, when the hostage-taking occurred. After it ended, she continued to work there until mid-August, when she quit her job to return to university to continue her studies.

On that fateful morning of June 9, J.W. was scooped up and herded down to Room 9 along with the other hostages. She didn't recognize any of the inmate hostage-takers. Initially, she was "pretty shaky," and one hostage told her to sit down until the rest of the hostages came in. At that point, "we were told eventually to go into the vault."

When the coroner asked, "During the daylight hours of June 9, the Monday, were you at any time subjected to any form of indignity or mistreatment at all?"

J.W. replied, "No."

"Were you at any time—were there any threats made to you directly?" the coroner asked.

"No."

J.W. continued to speak of the atmosphere in the vault on that first day. "It was very tense and very hot." She admitted that her memory of the whole thing was very vague. "It's hard for me to distinguish between days. I can remember different events," she continued, "but I can't remember that such and such happened on a particular day."

Had she seen Mary frequently during that time?

"No," J.W. replied, "because Mary was out in front of the vault in Room 9." Only once or possibly twice, she was told to relieve Mary for a couple of hours. On one of those occasions, she explained, Dwight was armed with

---

44 J.W.'s witness testimony taken from the *Proceedings of the Inquest on the Death of Maria Elizabeth Steinhauser*, Booklet IX, 4–51.

a knife—one that came dangerously close to her throat. "...he [Lucas] sat directly behind me and held the knife fairly close towards my throat."

"When you say 'very closely,' could you feel it at any time? Was it touching your neck?" the coroner asked.

"Yeah, I—it was in the evening and I remember very distinctly going—sort of nodding off and hitting the knife, which would wake me up."

At one point, as Mary and J.W. were washing their hands in the vault. "We were talking about what was going on. Mary was telling me that everything was going to be all right." She (Mary) spoke to me "in a reassuring and compassionate tone."

Although much of the forty-one hours were a blur, J.W. recalled very clearly "the part just before we broke out...I can remember talking to Mary before she went out for the last time. I can remember having a conversation with Mr. W., and I can remember hearing about the plans to break out....I was told maybe five minutes beforehand by Mr. Z., that there was a plan to break out."

What was her reaction to this news? the coroner asked.

She replied that she was in favour of it, but that she was very scared.

It was only minutes later when several male hostages took matters into their own hands. The time seemed ripe to act. Claire Wilson was inside the vault but apparently in a drug-induced torpor and unlikely to prove a challenge to what would happen next.

The men tried to slowly pull the vault door closed from within, but failing to do so, they smashed a camera tripod over the head of Dwight Lucas, who was on the outside trying to keep the door open. But Dwight didn't fall down and instead began wildly stabbing the knife through the opening in the door.

Everyone was screaming and yelling, including J.W. She couldn't see anything that was happening at the vault door because she was in one of the bays of the vault, with no sightline to the door.

Suddenly, she heard thuds against the door and somebody said, "Those are bullets or something like that."

Then someone from outside said, "Open the door," and when they did somebody took her hand and said, "'Just walk through here,' and I saw...

The person who took my hand said not to look—I saw blood on the wall and I just didn't look."

When it was time for the jurors to question J.W., she was asked if she knew Mary fairly well. "I only knew her through my office."

"Would you say she [Mary] was a very compassionate individual?" the juror asked.

"Yes."

"Extremely so?"

"Yes."

The coroner wanted to clarify something a juror had posed to J.W. "You stated, Mrs. W., that Miss Steinhauser was compassionate, and in answer to one of the juror's questions about hostility you said, 'Not to me.' Did you ever witness her to be hostile towards anyone?"

"Not hostile, but she believed in standing up for what she believed in, and I imagine that some people didn't like that. I know that in staff meetings if she disagreed with anything, she was extremely verbal—verbal about it and would let her opinions be known."

At this point, J.W. made an interesting observation about the gender bias of the inmates against the male hostages. The two women hostages in the vault (herself and Louise Stratton[45]) had a much easier time of it that the male hostages. As J.W. recalled, Dwight "took each male hostage around to the third bay area and said—punched them and said, you know, that if they didn't keep in line, that he would—they would get more of this or something to that effect."

I silently waited for J.W. to continue. I desperately wanted to hear an answer to my question, "Why did the hostages inside the vault take such a dreadful chance to break out knowing that Mary was outside and so vulnerable…so painfully vulnerable?"

And then this came from an inmate's lawyer:

> LAWYER: Could you tell me why you were in favour of it [the breakout plan]? What made you think that this was the thing to do at this time?

---

45   Classification officer who was held hostage in the vault along with the thirteen other hostages.

J.W.: Because I didn't feel that we were getting too much support from the Penitentiary Service or whoever was—was supposedly arranging things. I also was afraid that one of the male hostages was going to be killed.

I held my breath as he continued his line of questioning.

LAWYER: Were you able to think at that time about—first of all, were you aware that Miss Steinhauser was still outside in the room?

J.W.: Yes, I was.

LAWYER: Did any thoughts go through your mind as to her position or what might occur to her?

J.W.: I think we talked about it and I think that we both agreed that the inmates certainly wouldn't hurt her.

When it was my turn to question J.W., I asked her about the staff meeting in which Mary was very vocal in expressing her opinions. What exactly had the meetings been about? Did she feel that the meetings or the matter under discussion at the meetings were not terribly important?

J.W. nodded in agreement.

MARGARET: Why did you feel that way?

J.W.: I think that a lot of the meetings sort of centered around bureaucracy and red tape and not about what was happening to inmates.

MARGARET: What would you say was Mary's main concern?

Her answer was quick and unequivocal.

J.W.: Inmates and their rights.

CORONER: I think it's been made abundantly clear by J.W., in her own opinion and her own observations, that Miss Steinhauser was a determined individual obviously and didn't make any bones about making her views apparent to others. Was she [Mary] upset about the lack of rights or too many rights [for the inmates]?

J.W.: Lack of rights.

CORONER: Lack of rights for the inmates?

J.W.: Murmured agreement.

The next questioner was a juror who attempted to understand why the hostages felt the inmates wouldn't hurt Mary.

JUROR: I suppose that in your discussion you mentioned that you didn't— you and another hostage didn't think that they would hurt Mary because of her feelings towards the inmates. I suppose that was the reason that you didn't think that they would hurt her. Was that correct or…

J.W.: I just didn't think that they would hurt her.

JUROR: Because of her feelings towards the inmates?

J.W.: I think that they had a great deal of respect towards her.

Still further on in her testimony, J.W. was asked by the coroner about her knowledge of the special correction units (also known as Solitary Confinement Units or SCUs) at the B.C. Penitentiary and asked her to describe them for the jury's benefit.

"It was pretty shocking," she replied when asked about the first time she saw one. "The room was very bare, cement. It's somewhere where somebody has to live—I forget—they get two hours of exercise if that a day or so; it's somewhere where they're spending most of their day in there. My memory of it was that it was cement and this was where they were living with very little—"

"And your impression was one of what? Horror as opposed to disgust?" the coroner asked.

"I was shocked."

The coroner repeated her response for affirmation. "Shocked?"
"I was shocked."
A juror continued to seek more clarity on the nature of the SCUs.

> JUROR: I'd just like to know whether in your opinion this hostage incident occurred because of this SCU situation. So you think that was the—What precipitated it? So you think that was the reason for it solely?
>
> J.W.: All three of them had spent a great deal of time in the SCU area, and they were saying that unless you've been up there, you just don't know what it's like."
>
> LAWYER FOR THE INMATES: Was there tension, I mean something like an inherent tension that came from inherent conflicts in the job between security and classification officers?
>
> J.W.: I felt it with some of the custody officers. I found some of them were very rude, very uncooperative. Some of them were very polite and very co-operative. It was just the individual.

Soon after, the coroner finished his questioning and allowed J.W. to stand down. I watched her as she slowly made her way out of the courtroom, free to go home to a spouse, possibly children or a family. She was free. Her ordeal was over, and I was glad for her. She seemed like a good and kind person.

But what cruel twist of fate it was that denied my sister only a year before, the undeniable pleasure and comfort of doing exactly what J.W. was about to do now.

To walk away, to be free to go home.

I pondered this for some time.

Next on the witness stand was one John Ryan, classification officer.[46] Taunted and tormented throughout their forty-one hours of captivity by inmate Dwight Lucas, Ryan had been singled out for the worst treatment

---

46 John Ryan's witness testimony taken from the *Proceedings of the Inquest on the Death of Maria Elizabeth Steinhauser*, Booklet VIII, 79–105.

of all the hostages who escaped alive from the vault that early morning in June.

After being sworn in, Ryan, a man in his early forties, began his testimony by describing his employment situation a year after the hostage-taking. Although he was still employed by the federal government, he revealed that his physical and emotional trauma were so deep that he'd been on medical leave for a full year, with physician's orders never to return to work in any penal institute.

Acknowledging the severity of Ryan's emotional state, the coroner cautioned counsel to make their questions to Ryan very short and to the point throughout his testimony.

> CORONER: Where were you, Mr. Ryan, during the early morning hours of June 9, 1975?
>
> RYAN: I was talking to Mary just prior to the hostage incident—Mary Steinhauser.
>
> CORONER: In which room?
>
> RYAN: I was in Mary's office. We were looking at some pictures I had taken the previous two weeks…of one of the clubs that she was associated with.
>
> CORONER: You mean still photographs.
>
> RYAN: Yes. I had taken some pictures of the group, and she had got the pictures back on the weekend and we were examining them about quarter to eight in the morning.
>
> CORONER: I see. When you say the group, which group are you referring to?
>
> RYAN: One of the groups that she was liaison person for. I can't quite remember the name of the group now, but Chief Dan George came in and was a guest speaker there… It was just some kind of a community relations group, I think it was called.

CORONER: And as you were talking with Miss Steinhauser in her office, what happened?

RYAN: I had just left her office and returned to mine, and inmate Lucas came along and just grabbed hold of me with a knife in his hand.

Was he seized physically? the coroner pressed on.

Yes, grabbed by the shirt-front by inmate Dwight Lucas, a man he'd never seen before. Ryan described Dwight as wearing a pair of gloves and holding a long, thin-bladed knife, like a filleting knife, which he held up to Ryan's throat. He tried to make a break for it, but Dwight held on, and Ryan was pushed down the steps and eventually into the vault, where all the other hostages were already being held.

What happened next struck terror into the hearts of the hostages.

RYAN: We had received threats and told that we—it was a similar situation to the Attica affair,[47] the Attica—

CORONER: Attica?

RYAN: Yeah, that there'd be lots of deaths and they made several points about—

The coroner interrupted, asking for clarification as to who "they" were. It was all three inmates who made the threats, Ryan continued: Andy Bruce, whom he knew well because Andy was on his caseload, and Dwight Lucas and Claire Wilson, neither of whom he knew or recognized. All three also made pointed comments about "the fact that they were wearing gloves so that when they stabbed or cut us, the knives wouldn't slip in their hands."

I listened raptly as Ryan described the reign of terror.

---

47 Attica, or the Attica Prison uprising, which occurred at the Attica Correctional Facility in Attica, New York, over a four-day period September 9–13, 1971. One of the most significant uprisings of the prisoners' rights movement, it was based on prisoners' demands for improved living conditions and political rights. Over 1,200 prisoners took control of the prison taking forty-two staff hostage. When the uprising was over, at least forty-three people were dead, including ten correctional officers and civilian employees, and thirty-three inmates.

After the inmates asked the prison personnel for drugs, the hostages had to stand with their hands over their heads while inmates stripped them of all their personal belongings, their rings, watches, jewelry, shoes, wallets, or anything that would ID them, the latter so that "we couldn't be identified if we were killed."

Shortly after, Lucas asked the administration for manacles, handcuffs, and leg irons to restrain the hostages. The administration refused.

All the while, inside the vault, Lucas and Wilson were doing most of the talking to the hostages while Andy was negotiating with the prison personnel outside in Room 9. At some point, Lucas told the anxious hostages "that approximately nine of the hostages would be taken out, with white sheets and pillowcases over us, all of us, nine hostages and three inmates manacled and handcuffed together to get into the plane or whatever transport was provided."

Other indignities and abuse followed.

At some point between eight and nine in the morning on that first day, Lucas singled Ryan out and poured some mercurochrome[48] from a first-aid kit over his head. Some of the mercurochrome leaked into Ryan's eyes, causing an acute stinging sensation and subsequent eye damage, which persisted a year later. As if that weren't enough, Lucas also sprayed him in the face with a kind of fly spray.

The abuse went on…Lucas kicked Ryan repeatedly, forced him to take overdoses of tranquillizers, stuck a knife dangerously close to his eyeball and in his ear, and took him into the corner of the vault and kicked him in the groin. Anytime there was a noise, Lucas would thrust his fist into Ryan's chest and put the knife to his throat saying, "Anything happens, you're the first to go."

Over and over for the entire forty-one hours, Lucas repeated his threat to Ryan. "Anything happens, you're the first to go."

Why was Ryan the target for this toxic abuse from Lucas? Ryan was clearly perplexed. "I had never seen Lucas in my life before. Never even

---

48 Trademark for a mercury-containing compound, sometimes known as the stinging antiseptic, used as an anti-bacterial antiseptic for treating wounds. Declared unsafe by the USFDA in 1998 because it contained mercury, it was banned in the United States.

heard of his name. The only one of the three I knew was [Andy] Bruce and he was on my caseload for some time."

Although all of the hostages must have suffered emotional wounds in the aftermath of their confinement, for Ryan there were visible wounds as well, specifically because of his harassment by Lucas. As a result of being hit in the chest, he had to have surgery for a hiatus hernia. Because his eyes were swollen for three months after the event, he needed to have eye surgery and was required to wear bifocals continuously thereafter.

On occasion, Dwight Lucas and Claire Wilson would threaten all the hostages.

"There were several threats made against myself and all of the hostages that they had cans of gasoline and they could set fire to us all besides knifing a few of us."

On Monday afternoon, Ryan was forced to take more tranquillizers. "Several times during the day I was given more tranquillizers and every time I tried to doze off, I was kicked by Lucas. He didn't want to see me sleeping, I guess, so—and—oh, our hands were tied, too, I believe it was Monday afternoon and Wilson and Lucas found some string in the vault and they tied up all of the male hostages."

Attempting to clarify the movement of the inmates during the first day of their confinement, the coroner posed a question to Ryan. "Was there a steady stream coming and going of the inmates in and out of the vault area?"

"Wilson would pop out once in a while and Lucas popped out once in a while, but basically I think that they were in most of the time and Bruce was outside with Mary most of the time."

As I listened to Ryan speak, I grew increasingly agitated and felt the mounting sense of foreboding that all the hostages must have felt as time dragged on. They knew every action or reaction they made might tip the volatile Lucas into some dangerously fatal response.

But somehow, the night passed.

It was Tuesday morning.

> CORONER: During the Tuesday, what was going on during the Tuesday morning again as far as you're concerned, Mr. Ryan?

RYAN: Well, first thing Tuesday morning, I had to go to the bathroom and there was a bucket in the vault, which was kind of full at this time and Lucas at knifepoint said I had to empty the thing out into the outer room there. What did you say? It was room 9? At this time I think a portable commode had been installed in there and I tipped the bucket in to the portable commode and as I was tipping it, I noticed that all of our jewelry and stuff was in the bottom of the bucket and I said to Lucas about it and he said, 'Keep on tipping, man. Just keep on tipping' so there was all the jewelry, the rings, watches, everything, wallets, everything that belonged to the hostages so it was tipped into the portable commode.

CORONER: Did you suffer any more physical abuse?

RYAN: A few more kicks once in a while when I tried to doze off and every time there was any kind of negotiations going I was grabbed by the shirt and a knife was put in my throat.

CORONER: Did you try to reason with this man at all?

RYAN: Verbally, no. I grabbed his hand on one occasion when he put the knife into my eye and he said, 'let go' so I let go.

At some point during Tuesday afternoon, there was a terrifying episode in the vault.
Claire Wilson lost his knife.
All three inmates became very hostile, threatening, and all the hostages were "kind of terrified of what was going to happen because of the missing knife…That was pretty dicey for a while because he [Wilson] came in and I thought somebody was going to show us how we were going to get it."
"Were you terrified?"
"Yes, sure. I think that was one of the most terrifying moments of all."
Eventually the knife was located in the vault, and Wilson reclaimed it.
The day wore on, and at around 7:00 p.m. on Tuesday evening, Ryan was woozy but worried that he would be in for some more severe abuse. Some of the hostages suggested, "Why don't you try to get under the table? We'll throw a blanket over you and maybe he'll [Lucas] forget about you

for a while." At which point, the exhausted man crawled under the table and someone threw a blanket over him, covering him from head to toe.

Ryan went to sleep.

Suddenly he heard shouts. Strange tapping noises coming from the vault door.

"I pulled myself up from under the table and all of the hostages were around the door shouting and screaming and I walked towards the door and the conversation was 'Who's on the outside of the door? Is it the inmates? Is it the guards? Who is it?' And the door opened and we dashed out."

Ryan was the last one out of the vault and into the night air; he fled through a phalanx of security, split on both sides like a corridor for the hostages to run through. From there he went into the director's office where all the other hostages were gathered. It was here that Ryan and his colleagues stayed for the next two or three hours as they tried to make sense of the horror they'd just endured.

Now that Ryan had finished answering the coroner's questions, the time had come for questioning by the interested parties, me included. I waited impatiently for the lawyers to finish their questions. I had one question on my mind for Ryan. What did he remember about the pictures he took at the Community Awareness Day?

I was especially interested in making it very clear that the now infamous, much discussed picture of Mary and Andy Bruce, standing side by side, which some unknown person had released to the *Vancouver Sun* newspaper and was subsequently published on the front page of the Wednesday, January 21, 1976, edition was *not* the only picture of Andrew Bruce with his arm around a woman. In my possession, I had a photo of a large group of people taken at that same Community Awareness Day, in which Andy Bruce had his arm around another female.

So I began my questioning.

> MARGARET: I wonder if you could tell me in relation to the picture you took of Mary and Andy—Andy Bruce—do you also recall taking a picture, a large group picture, where Mary was standing at one end—it was a large group and in the middle was standing Andy—Andrew Bruce with his arm around another unidentified female?

RYAN: Yeah, I took about a hundred pictures and I couldn't tell you the composition of each one by no means. There may have been ten pictures with Bruce with his arm around somebody, I don't know. I haven't seen the pictures and I don't know where they are.

Possibly ten pictures of Bruce with his arm around somebody? Ten pictures? I mused

MARGARET: You don't recall taking that particular picture?

RYAN: I took several group pictures and I could have taken ten with Bruce with his arm around a girl, but I—

MARGARET: Was he, in fact, standing with his arm around any other girl at any other time in those pictures taken?

RYAN: I took about a hundred pictures and most of them were in links with their arms around girlfriends, wives, females generally. I didn't pay that much attention to Bruce so I couldn't tell you.

And there it was…from the photographer himself the explanation that most of the pictures taken at that event were of inmates and guests mingling freely and of inmates having their pictures taken with female guests or staff.

So the fact that some unknown person with malevolent intent to slander Mary's reputation had found this photo and released it "surreptitiously" (as described by the coroner) to the press was now firmly established in the record.

"Thank you very much," I said and sat down.

18

MARKSMAN

*In summary, there were **eight** shots fired in all.*
They were as follows:
An officer, using a four-inch .38, fired two shots at
Bruce and one at Lucas. Total: three.
An officer, using a four-inch .38, fired two shots at Bruce
and one shot at Lucas. Total: three.
An officer, using a four-inch .38 Smith & Wesson,
fired one shot at Bruce. Total: one.
An officer, using a four-inch .38, accidentally discharged one shot.
Total: one.[49]

WITNESS TESTIMONY OF DR. FREDERICK STURROCK, PATHOLOGIST[50]

Coroner's inquest—May 26, 1976

CORONER: Did you perform a post-mortem examination on a deceased identified to you as Mary Steinhauser?

Dr. S.: Yes I did, on the 11th of June, 1975, at, I think, 11:15 hours, and the body was that of a young, white female appearing the stated age of thirty-two years. The body measured sixty-seven inches in

---

49 *Report of the Commission of Inquiry*, 33.
50 Witness testimony booklet I, 6–7.

length and weighed an estimated 125 pounds. There were two gunshot wounds of entrance, the first measuring approximately a quarter inch in diameter and somewhat oval in outline. It entered three inches to the left and two inches above the manubrial notch, which is the notch in the top of the sternum or the breast bone. It passed backwards and downwards over a distance of about four inches and exited through the skin at a point one inch below the wound of entrance and four inches behind it.

CORONER: That would commonly be known as a flesh wound, is that right?

Dr. S.: Yes, flesh wound. There was a second wound of entrance situated in the left chest, three inches to the left and five inches below the manubrial notch. This wound penetrated through the skin and the underlying tissue and angled from the left side of the deceased to the right slightly. It went through the breast bone at approximately the middle portion, roughly at the level of where the fifth costal cartilage joins the bone. That's somewhere in the lower half of the breast bone. It went through the right main chamber of the heart. It went through the—it came out through the right atrium, which is the small chamber above the main chamber of the heart. It went through the lower portion of the right lung. It penetrated the muscles on the inner portion of the chest wall at the back and it hit the eighth rib posteriorly—that is at the back—one inch to the right of the vertebral column, that is the bony spine, and the bullet was recovered in the muscles between the eighth and ninth rib at the back.

...

There was no evidence of any pre-existing disease of any significance, and death was due to a gunshot wound of the chest, which penetrated the heart and the right lung with massive bleeding therefrom.

Today was June 29, and for one full month I'd listened to witness after witness as they described what they saw, heard, did, thought, said, or felt, before and during those forty-one hours over a year before, when time stood still and the world watched and waited. Waited, that is, for some kind of peaceful outcome to the standoff between three desperate inmates holding fifteen hostages in a vault within the B.C. Penitentiary and the penitentiary staff who were charged with monitoring an extremely volatile and dangerous situation which could turn deadly at any minute.

In the early hours of the hostage-taking, the penitentiary officials made a quick decision to form an armed assault team composed of their own correctional officers. This tactical team, or squad as it came to be known, was charged with the responsibility of acting with force

a. if the hostages themselves attempted a breakout, or

b. if there was a hostile action of an inmate towards a hostage.

Mostly untrained in hostage-taking situations, and with no prior experience working together as a team or in a situation of such magnitude, this in-house emergency response team was hastily assembled and chosen based on their skills and expertise as marksmen. Five of the members were ex-policemen or ex-military personnel.

All six members of this fledgling assault team gave testimony at the inquest, but two of the members were of particular interest to me. Why? Because these two men had considerable facility handling firearms and were considered expert marksmen. Moreover, they had fired three shots each at Bruce and Lucas, for a total of six shots.

The first was Albert Hollinger, marksman.

Named by Chief Justice Farris in the Commission of Inquiry as the reason why "it will never be ascertained who shot and killed Mary Steinhauser," Albert Hollinger was the man responsible for a "coverup" in which Justice Farris "accused Hollinger of intentionally failing to make a record of which gun was used by which guard in the June 11 guards' assault." Farris added that "Hollinger had 'mixed up' the guns so it would never be possible to determine who fired the fatal shot at Miss Steinhauser." In issuing his finding, Farris angrily rejected as "completely unacceptable" and "unbelievable" and "an insult to our intelligence" an explanation that had been given by Hollinger during an earlier and closed session of the inquiry as to why he had not recorded which guard had used which gun.[51]

However, before Hollinger was to testify tomorrow, we would hear from Officer Y., another marksman and member of interest to me.

Today I would hear about the final seconds in the early morning hours of June 11 when, at hearing shouts and screams from Room 9, the squad raced down the hallway of the classification building with their guns at the ready. Leading this final charge was Officer Y., who arrived at the upper half of the Dutch door only moments before his teammate, Albert Hollinger.

I leaned forward, listening intently as Officer Y. began to speak.

OFFICER Y.[52] testifies

At thirty years of age, Officer Y. was currently employed at the B.C. Penitentiary as a corrections officer and had been for six years, since 1970. His work put him in contact with many inmates, he said, and he'd worked in all the ranks over the years.

With some considerable pride, Officer Y. said he was a marksman. Shooting wasn't just a skill he needed for work, it was his hobby. The coroner wanted information about his training.

> CORONER: Let's dwell a moment on your training as a marksman. What type of training have you had in the way of use and handling of firearms, particularly small arms?
>
> Y.: I've—I suppose—I've had lots of training, but—I tea—I've taught it. I presently teach it. Revolver. I do a lot of shooting in competitions. I travel around quite a bit. It's my hobby.
>
> CORONER: Do you belong to a gun club?
>
> Y.: Yes, sir.
>
> CORONER: That's totally divorced from the Penitentiary Service?

---

51 Alex Young, "Deliberate coverup charged", Vancouver BC, Province, July 26, 1975.
52 Witness testimony booklet XIV, 81–180.

Y.: Oh, yes. I belong to a Law Enforcement Shooter Association, which is strictly police officers that compete once a month on our range, and there's always matches all over.

...

CORONER: What about the—where did you learn or pick up the art of shooting a firearm? It's no mean task?

Y.: As a—as a boy, I had a .22 like every kid did back on the farm.

CORONER: That's a rifle you're speaking of?

Y.: Right. Were you asking revolver?

CORONER: Yes.

Y.: I'm sorry. I went to school in '71 that they hold—it's changed now, but that they held at that time for induction officers—training of officers when you first come into the employment of the Penitentiary Service. You spend some time in the institutions and then they send you on a nine-week or twelve-week course and there was very little, but that was where I was introduced to revolvers. Half a day, we did some practice and we had a bit of—two or three lectures—hour lectures in the classroom, I guess.

The coroner asked him if he'd done much range shooting.

Y.: No, sir. Just about three years ago, I started—it was in September, in fact, three years ago. I started my—I went to my first match and you learn as you go. We shoot at paper targets. They're black. They don't have a bull's eye–type thing on them.

CORONER: How about moving targets?

Y.: Not with a revolver. I've shot shotgun with a clay pigeon, but not with a revolver. The only time they'd ever move is sometimes the targets are in a rack—in a stand and they're on edge. You can't see them and you're clued to go or to fire into the time frame. They turn the target. It's mechanically or electrically done, but that's all it does. It doesn't go from left to right. It just goes 180 degrees.

Officer Y. continued with his recounting of the forty-one hours.

That early spring morning on June 9, 1975 held great promise for Officer Y. because his status in the Canadian Penitentiary Service was about to change for the better. At 8:00 a.m., he was reporting to his new position as a staff instructor for the Instructional Staff College, the training arm for the Canadian Penitentiary Service.

He'd come to the Pen an hour early, intending to finish typing up a report for a colleague. He was almost done when a call came in from a clearly agitated supervisor, directing him to take over the phones and call all the shop instructors to return the inmates back to the cell block. A hostage situation was underway!

After quickly following orders, Officer Y. was ordered to report to the front gate area where he was given a telescopic rifle in a rifle case. His superior had requested a 'rifleman,' and Mr. Y., having considerable experience in firearms training, was an obvious choice.

Over the next few hours, various iterations of the size and composition of the tactical squad were tried and discarded. At approximately 10:00 p.m. on the evening of the first day, it was settled that a six-man squad would suffice. All the members of the squad were ensconced in Room 15, a very small room about fifty feet down the hallway from Room 9 where Mary was with Andy Bruce and where, beyond that, Dwight Lucas and the other fifteen hostages were in the adjoining vault with inmate Claire Wilson.

The squad was to be as close as possible to this room but out of both sight and hearing of the inmates. They were given two directives: they were allowed only to enter the area

a. if the hostages were attempting to break out, *or*

b. if the inmates were attacking the hostages.

Over the next twenty-four hours, the squad moved from room to room, trying to find a room sufficiently spacious for six men and their weapons and at a discreet distance from Room 9. They finally ended up Room 202, approximately 150 feet from Room 9 and the adjoining vault.

It was now midnight on the night of June 10. The night was going to be a quiet one, Officer Y. said. They'd been reassured that they wouldn't be needed anymore that night. "'Till morning,' they said. 'Get some sleep if you can.' The guys unloaded everything, stuck it on the table. The weapons were loaded, but the cylinders were open. Batons, holsters, and all that type of stuff was there…"

Suddenly at around 1:00 a.m., Officer Y. "heard some awful screaming—terrible screaming, and I got up and I hollered to the guys, 'Let's go!' and I grabbed a weapon and I ran down the hallway."

When he arrived at the Dutch door to Room 9, Officer Y. looked in. "The first thing I saw was Bruce holding Mary. He was holding her with a left arm around him—around her. She was slumped over and she appeared to be unconscious or fainted or whatever."

I questioned his story—*how could Mary be unconscious?*

She hadn't been stabbed, hit, punched, or harmed in any way by either Andy Bruce or Lucas.

Nor could she be unconscious as a result of taking a small amount of Noludar, a mild tranquilizer, a few hours earlier in the evening. The toxicology report by the pathologist established that the Noludar was "a really inconsequential" amount at ".05 mgm percent in the blood. The normal therapeutic dose, that is the dose that one would expect to produce a reasonable effect if you were using it medically, is about 1 mg percent, so this is only one-twentieth of a therapeutic dose and the lethal level is up around three or more."

Officer Y. continued his story, his voice rising as he described Bruce's motions. "He [Andy] had that big knife and it was sitting right here [indicating]. His hand was over his head."

Then Y. saw "what appeared to be blood right here, on her breast area, and the knife was right here [indicating] in the breast bone area."

He yelled at Bruce to freeze. "I just said 'Freeze' and then I said, 'Bruce, drop the knife.'" Officer Y. was convinced that Andy Bruce had heard him say "Freeze!" but unsure if Andy had actually heard him hear the second utterance, "Bruce, drop the knife!" because just at that moment, there was a big noise, a loud noise from the area to his left.

Moments later, aiming at Bruce, he "fired two hands, single action, which means you cock the revolver to the rear and I aimed right there and I fired."

Seconds later, Officer Y. fired again at Bruce. "I think that I—I believe I hit him."

His final shot was aimed at Lucas. "By this time, Bruce and Mary had dropped down and were hidden from view by the couch. Lucas was facing the vault door. He had a long, slender knife and it was that high [indicating]. He was standing fully erect and he was heading toward the vault door."

So he shot at Lucas, "aiming for his temple. And Lucas dropped like he'd been hit with an axe."

Once inside Room 9, Officer Y. "walked across the tables and—'cause there was tables solid, and Bruce was down, Mary was in his arms and there was blood all over the place."

I took a deep breath and steeled myself to listen to Officer Y.'s account of Mary's last seconds.

"Hudson and I got Mary out into the hall and we couldn't get a stretcher for her. The hall was cluttered up and the stretchers were coming, but we couldn't get her—and she just inhaled and exhaled and then we laid her on the ground and that was—I left Mary. Hudson stayed with her and I went back and I picked up the knives, both knives."

Officer Y. had fired three shots, twice in the direction of Bruce and once in the direction of Lucas. He was shocked when he heard Mary had been killed as a result of a gunshot wound and not stabbed, as everyone had first believed.

His testimony almost over, it was my turn to ask my question. "Just one more question. Mr. Y., do you think that any one of the bullets that you fired actually entered Mary's body?"

"I don't believe so, but anything's possible because with the situation, anything's possible. I can miss—like I said before, I could miss that doorknob in conditions not being right. I don't think so in my own mind and I hope to God not, but I don't think so."

But I thought you were a marksman, I whispered silently to myself.

It was now June 30, the second to last day of the inquest, and the day before the Canada Day long weekend. I'd waited for a very long time for this moment.

It had been more than a year since one Albert Hollinger, corrections officer, had been publicly chastised by the Farris Commission because he'd tampered with vital evidence. It had been one year since I learned that he had obscured forever the physical evidence of which guard had held the gun that fired the fatal shot that killed my sister.

I wanted to see this man, to confront him with the reality of what he'd done.

Hollinger was now seated in the witness stand. The lawyer for the penitentiary personnel hastened to describe the considerable strain and abuse Hollinger had been subject to since the incident had occurred.

"He is presently under medical care. He is not working. There have been death threats against him, both inside and outside the institution. There has been an extortion attempt through the mail informing him that unless he did certain things, a contract would be taken out on his life. These matters have been reported to the RCMP. They have been reported to the police force within the jurisdiction where he resided. I may say further that since this incident occurred, his daughter has had to leave school. Both he and his wife have had medical attention and, of course, it goes without saying that he has a problem with any friends coming to visit him in his home. I think those matters should be brought to the Court's attention. He is still under medical attention and under a good deal of strain. I might say that there have been a number of allegations made against him by a number of different people. Certainly there have been statements made by inmates which prompted this type of difficulty that this man has had. He has certainly been the target of a good deal of abuse."[53]

Although Hollinger was still employed at the B.C. Pen, he wasn't actually working at the time because he was under compensation.

---

53 Witness testimony booklet XV, 81.

ALBERT HOLLINGER testifies[54]

Describing his status on June 9, 1975, as that of a correctional officer CX6 at the B.C. Penitentiary, Albert Hollinger, forty-three, began his testimony.

Was he a marksman? the coroner asked.

With a kind of smug immodesty, Hollinger quickly reeled off a virtual shopping list of awards for marksmanship he'd received in his lifetime. By the time he finished, I was convinced his love of guns was not just a part of his job, it was his hobby and his obsession. The first award, his crowning achievement, was earning the title of Lifetime Master at the National Rifle Association of America, the highest award given covering all firearms, which the most prestigious of all rifle association bestows on only its most gifted of riflemen. The second was the classification of Master in Canada, the highest award given for Canadian marksmen. Furthermore, to attain these two classifications one had to shoot 1,448 out of 1,500 in competition, regularly.

He also belonged to the Law Enforcement Shooting Association, having joined in June 1974. At least once a month, if not twice, he would enter into competitions and attend shooting events. In 1974 and 1975, he'd won the Canadian Penitentiary Service National Championship for revolver. In 1975, he won the Regional Championship for revolver and rifle. He'd also won the silver shield in Dominion Marksman for both handguns and rifles in the early '50s.

Surprisingly, his next revelation was that he was a gunsmith. Serving an apprenticeship early on in his life, Hollinger became a gunsmith running a home-based business, mostly moonlighting, for six years.

As if that weren't enough to convince the members of the courtroom of Hollinger's love of gun culture, he added that "I was in the army and I was head of our platoon, the 37th Field Regiment," which meant "I was the best shot with the rifle and the 9mm automatic."

But it was Hollinger's next act that I found chilling.

---

54 Witness testimony booklet XV, 82–177.

It followed the coroner's question: "And those three shots[55] you fired off, was it always in rest position?"

"Rest position. I didn't even move. I just fired the gun. I was down like this crouched and I fired the gun and I just swung like that." As he lowered his body over the desk, Hollinger stretched out his arm, positioning his finger and thumb like a revolver. He looked down towards his outstretched hand, with its make-believe weapon, as if he were capturing some virtual target in its crosshairs.

Clearly, he was enjoying the opportunity to demonstrate his superior marksmanship to his captive courtroom audience. It was an eerily disturbing sight, and one I'll never forget.

Did Hollinger know of Andy, Dwight, and Claire prior to that morning? the coroner asked.

"I've had dealings with them," Hollinger replied. And further, he had had reason to "discipline all three of them as was his duty to do." They were, all three of them, Hollinger declared, "found guilty as charged."

After the tactical squad was assembled, Hollinger met up with four other corrections officers and other security personnel, where they collectively began to formulate some sort of plan as to what they were going to do. But they weren't given much direction, and "for the first four or five hours there was really not much laid on, it seemed. We were just waiting."

Finally, they decided to move to a very small room in the classification building, which was close to Room 9. While sequestered in this seven by nine foot room, Hollinger's main concern was to keep their position as secret as possible from the inmates.

"We took all our stuff out of our pockets. We ran around in bare feet. We kept our voices to a whisper. The phone rang a couple of times but we didn't dare answer it for fear that the inmates were phoning all of the rooms and we would run into problems that way."

For the next twenty-four hours, the six men stayed in that room. They were so close to Room 9 that "we could hear the inmates talking."

It was now midnight on June 10.

---

55 Hollinger admitted to firing three shots, two in the direction of Bruce and one in the direction of Lucas.

Everything was quiet in Room 9, and it seemed there would be no further action that night. So the staff person, acting as a kind of sentry at the Dutch door and messenger, came into their room and motioned for them to vacate the room and "get out and try and relax. We're going to wait until morning."

With that, all six men crept out, one and two at a time, down the hallway to Room 202, which was much larger and farther away from Room 9. There, they could "relax a bit, walk around, talk in a fairly normal voice…" Since none of the men had been able to sleep for the past forty hours, they welcomed the opportunity to lay down on a mattress and doze off.

Not for long, though.

Suddenly, from the doorway, Officer Y. commanded, "Come on, fellows, let's go."

Instantly awake, Hollinger was on his feet, hearing all kinds of commotion coming from down the corridor, "a lot of human, loud voices, screaming, yelling!" He grabbed his revolver and began running down the corridor, following Officer Y., who was some "thirty-five to fifty feet ahead of me going full blast."

Briefly changing his line of questioning, the coroner asked Hollinger about his knowledge of Mary. I listened closely. What would he say about Mary?

> CORONER: By the way, before we go any further, were you acquainted with Miss Mary Steinhauser?
>
> HOLLINGER: I had no dealings whatsoever with her, except to admit her in the front gate when I was in charge of it. That was the only discussions we carried on together, and that was just to ask her for ID to let her in the gate. I never knew her or had any meetings with her or any of this stuff.
>
> CORONER: I see. How about the other—did you know that she was a classification officer?
>
> ….
>
> HOLLINGER: Oh, I knew she was a classification officer. I mean,

I knew very few of them on a basis where we talked together. Just some of the older fellows that were there from before…

CORONER: Let's get down to the shooting itself. As you took up your positions, what, in your mind's eye, was going on, and before anyone said or did anything, what was going on in front of your very eyes?

HOLLINGER: I saw inmate Lucas crouched behind the chesterfield, a sofa-type thing. I could see his head and part of his shoulder. Now, in front of him, I saw what appeared to be a woman's hair and type of Hawaiian style dress of some sort. You know, very colourful clothing.

This statement of Hollinger's puzzled me. How could he see something as unlikely as that?

HOLLINGER: Now, he had one hand lying on the top of the chesterfield because the chesterfield's facing me, the back of it was towards the wall…This hand was resting on the couch like so [indicating] and it had that long skinny knife in it.

The next thing Hollinger heard was Officer Y. yelling "Freeze," and something else, which didn't register with him because he was intent on aiming at Lucas.

HOLLINGER: I brought the gun down like so [indicating]. This is the way I fire with one hand under. I rested it on the Dutch door top and fired a very, very quick shot at Lucas.

Dwight Lucas was down and he was gone, instantly. Hollinger then looked sideways at Andy Bruce and Mary.

HOLLINGER: Then the next thing I saw was Bruce standing with his left arm around Mary—

CORONER: Miss Steinhauser.

HOLLINGER: Miss Steinhauser—apparently unconscious.

CORONER: Who was unconscious?

HOLLINGER: Miss Steinhauser.

CORONER: How could you tell? What gave you that impression?

HOLLINGER: Okay, what gave me that impression was the same as—the police asked me the same thing. Her face was all drawn. Her lips were very close together. Her eyes were shut. Her face—that's the first thing I saw was her face.

CORONER: Could you see her whole face?

HOLLINGER: I could see all of her except maybe from the belt down. It was behind part of the chesterfield and part of something else that was there.

CORONER: Did you say her head was slumped forward?

HOLLINGER: No, sideways…He had his arm around her like this [indicating] and he had the knife in his right hand and it was up like this [indicating], maybe about a foot away from her neck or face area…

At this point, I could feel my throat muscles constricting, afraid to breathe and to hear Hollinger's telling of what may have been the shots that killed my sister.

Hollinger took aim and fired at Andy Bruce.

The minute he fired, Bruce staggered a bit, and his hand with the knife went straight up in the air. "Meanwhile, Mary was still—or Miss Steinhauser was still continuing to slump over at this time. She was slumping over sort of medium slowly all the time that this was taking place in these few seconds."

Seconds later, taking careful aim, Hollinger fired again at Bruce, because his arm with the knife in it was coming down and "his head, right shoulder, and right chest area were exposed. For a split second I figured I've got to do something, and I took careful aim and I aimed right here [indicating] because he has a fair amount of hair and I didn't want to go over top of it. I fired that shot and his face instantly became bloody. It just exploded in blood."

Momentarily shocked, I shuddered at Hollinger's graphic description of a face "exploding in blood."

Several minutes passed while the coroner wrapped up his questions.

It was now 4:25 p.m., and the cross-examination was about to begin. There was a momentary lull in the proceedings as the jurors and lawyers arranged their papers.

Suddenly, out of the corner of my eye, I saw a movement from the direction of the jury.

They were seated in front of me, all seven men chosen by the coroner to deliberate on the reasons for my sister's death. They'd grown restless, moving about in their seats, shifting position repeatedly. I saw the foreman glance several times at his watch, as if he were anxious to be relieved of his duty for the week.

Hollinger was the last witness before the inquest would adjourn for five days, coincidentally over the Dominion Day weekend.[56] One of the lawyers was leafing through his papers, attempting to locate a piece of information about which he wished to examine Hollinger.

What I saw then shook me to the core.

Reaching into his left-hand pocket, one of the jury members, a florid-faced, elderly gentleman, produced a roll of Life Savers. Tearing off the outer wrappings, he looked around and, with an apologetic half-smile, reached out to offer Hollinger a Life Saver.

It was at that moment, at 4:30 p.m. on Wednesday, June 30, that I lost any illusions I might have had about the inquest into my sister's death.

It was that display of casual indifference to the gravity of the proceedings, to the enormity of what had happened to my sister, to the importance of being objective, to what was really important here in this court…I saw how little importance they placed on discovering how and why the system had failed to protect Mary, rendering her forever voiceless.

I mulled this over.

---

[56] Dominion Day is the former name for what is now Canada Day, July 1.

A growing sense of despair arose within me, a feeling that time was running out, and that some critically important information was missing from the inquest and would never be revealed to the public.

Unless I spoke up.

What was it? Why was it so important to me? It was about Mary. About her essence. Her character.

Would I ever have the chance to reveal all I knew about her? Her passionate yet principled character, her outstanding bravery, her unique training and experiences as a psychiatric nurse, her time as a nurse at the Matsqui Institution, her understanding of narcotics addiction and mental health, her passionate defense of those who needed help and inspiration, her dogged determination to speak her mind, and her ultimate magnificent sacrifice?

This final point consumed me. I wanted the public to know why Mary, *had she been allowed to do so*, was exquisitely well-equipped to bring about a peaceful conclusion to the hostage-taking. Much more so than the six corrections officers making up the armed and inadequately trained tactical team. She had all the practical skills of a psychiatric nurse, coupled with her education as a social worker and a deep theoretical understanding of the sociological and cultural features of prison culture and the inmate experience.

So I asked the coroner for permission to present a statement of information about Mary on the following Tuesday, the final day of the inquest. It was in that statement that I would "bring to light some of her qualifications, etc., and give the court an opportunity to understand perhaps why she acted the way she did."

When asked what I meant by "acted the way she did," I explained that it would be a factual statement on her life/work experiences and her dedication.

To which the coroner replied, "There is nothing but good has been said about Miss Steinhauser."

Of course I knew differently. I replied, "I don't agree with you, Your Honour."

"Really, where did we miss out? Where did we miss out on this, Mrs. H.? Everyone who has been questioned about Miss Steinhauser has stated that she was extremely devoted to her job. She was a tough-minded individual, which is an admirable point in itself. She felt that what she was doing for the inmates in the penitentiary was a crusade on her part, and I can't recall anyone who would even attempt to impugn her memory or even her type of work or type of personality."

I shot back. It's about "various people during this inquest who are attempting or have attempted to imply, through questioning, that she was extremely lax, security wise, and that perhaps she even had a hand in it [the hostage-taking]. I really find that offensive."

Acknowledging there may have been implications, the coroner then deferred to the seven-man jury to make the decision about allowing me to speak.

The jury came back with the statement that they didn't feel my statement "would be relevant to her death, really."

At this point, one of the inmate's lawyers hastened to speak to my plea. "Mr. Coroner, I'd like to add one point. We've just heard in great detail before Mr. Hollinger's evidence, brought up by Mr. X., the strain, the threats, the extortion he received, his work history since the event, all of that is completely irrelevant to the death, but it has been brought out. This information, presumably, is before her death and I don't understand how what's happened to Mr. Hollinger since the incident that can be ruled relevant, when this [Margaret's statement of information] can't be."

I continued. "I'd like to introduce facts to indicate why she would maintain her composure throughout the incident and why, perhaps, if events were allowed to unfold, she might be alive today."

But the coroner declined, saying he "had to draw the line somewhere, Madame. We are dealing with sworn evidence from the witnesses giving their evidence. Now, as I said, I've allowed a tremendous amount of latitude in this that I don't normally allow at an inquest, but I know you've come out here from Toronto and have been extremely attentive. You haven't missed a session that we've had in this long, tedious inquest, but this is after the fact—we're talking about Mr. Hollinger and his medical treatment and so forth up to and including the time of the incident in which your sister, unfortunately, met her death."

I replied that a recent, very upsetting BCTV news segment had disturbed me because it suggested that "some people viewed Mary as having possibly been a partner in the hostage-taking."

But in spite of all my pleas to be heard and the one sole supporting voice from the inmate's lawyer, I could feel the forces stacked against me. It was clear. I could not bring any information about Mary forward to the court. Not now. Not ever.

I pondered this for a moment, but was interrupted by the coroner who asked, "Mrs. H., do you want to ask Mr. Hollinger any questions?"

So without any expectation that any more truths would emerge, I began to question Hollinger about his confidence in his ability and the abilities of the other members of the tactical squad to carry out their defined tasks. He replied that he had no doubts at all on either issue.

> HOLLINGER: I don't doubt my ability at all. I did carry out my orders exactly and explicitly as they were relayed to me. I didn't deviate one bit.

I pressed Hollinger further to find out if he had any concerns at all about the fact that a woman had died.

> MARGARET: Can I ask you if you felt any concern at any time about the fact that a woman had died?

> HOLLINGER: At that time I didn't know she was dead.

> MARGARET: When you knew she was dead?

> HOLLINGER: Well, I mean, I don't—

The coroner interjected his own question.

> CORONER: Was it upsetting to you, Mr. Hollinger, to know that this young woman was dead?

> HOLLINGER: Well, certainly it was.

Why did Hollinger have such difficulty in answering my question? It was as if he couldn't quite comprehend why his empathy, or lack of it, had anything to do with his really important job of maintaining the security of the facility.

> MARGARET: You were the first one to enter the vault after the shooting ended, is that correct?
>
> HOLLINGER: That's right.
>
> MARGARET: You observed the bodies touching each other in a semi-curled position on their sides. Did it occur to you to assist the two people who were obviously injured, possibly dead?
>
> HOLLINGER: My orders were to do what I did. There was [sic] other members to look after things like that.
>
> MARGARET: Didn't it occur to you at all to look at them and see if they needed help?
>
> HOLLINGER: Not at all, because if I stopped there then who was going to look after the vault. When you run a squad like that, you perform your duties as you're told to, otherwise you clash with other members who were assigned to assist the wounded.
>
> MARGARET: You mentioned that the entire siege was an "exciting time." Could you please define that?
>
> HOLLINGER: There was excitement in the air. There was lots of talk, which you couldn't understand because many people were talking at once. People were milling around.

Finally I asked Hollinger about being singled out for harassment.

> MARGARET: You've already mentioned that you have been singled out by the media for some unfortunate publicity and have been harassed as a result of this. Could you give any reason why you personally might have been singled out for harassment?

HOLLINGER: Well, partly because my name was publicized.

MARGARET: Do you think there's any justification at all?

HOLLINGER: None whatsoever. All I did was pick two guns up out of a group of seven.

MARGARET: To your knowledge then, Mr. Hollinger, did you kill Mary?

HOLLINGER: I know I didn't.

MARGARET: If you didn't do it, Mr. Hollinger, do you know who did?

HOLLINGER: I can't answer that question.

At that point, I ended my questioning of one Albert Hollinger, hardly listening to the remaining seemingly irrelevant questions of the jurors. What was the point? Hollinger was obviously bound by expectations of filial loyalty or professional agreement to maintain secrecy around the shooting. He would never tell.

I left the courtroom that afternoon with a heavy sense of foreboding. It would be five days before we would meet for the last time to hear the jury's verdict. What would the verdict be?

I took the bus that evening and then the ferry up to Sechelt to stay with my mom and dad. I would spend one last weekend with them before coming back to Vancouver the following Tuesday. After the inquest, I would return to my Toronto home. As the highway disappeared under the bus's fast-moving wheels, I pondered the outcome of this long and tortured inquest.

After six weeks during which the court met for sixteen days of inquest, after twenty-nine spoken testimonies, after 2,237 pages of recorded testimonies, after reliving for at least twenty-nine times the final days and hours before, during, and after Mary died, what truths would emerge? Would there be any?

I wondered and waited.

19
VERDICT

It was the afternoon of July 6, 1976. An expectant hush enveloped the courtroom, now in its final day of the inquest into Mary's death. The jurors were about to deliver their written verdict.[57] I leaned forward in my seat, intent on hearing every word.

"Mr. D.,[58] as foreman of the jury, have you reached a verdict, sir?"

"Yes, we have."

"Are you unanimous with your verdict?"

"Yes, we are."

The jury foreman handed over the verdict. In his deep, resonant voice, the coroner read out the verdict. "We, the undersigned jury, empanelled to enquire into the circumstances touching the death of Maria Elizabeth Steinhauser do find:

"That the said deceased was declared dead at 01:15 hours [1:15 a.m.] on the 11th day of June AD 1975 from injuries, to wit, gunshot wound of chest with penetration of heart and massive exsanguination[59] sustained when she, the said deceased, being an employee of the B.C. Penitentiary (Department of the Solicitor General of Canada) was shot on the date first mentioned in the said B.C. Penitentiary. We, the Jury, find that the death of Maria Elizabeth Steinhauser was unnatural and accidental."

Accidental? I gasped in shock. How could that be?

---

57 Witness testimony booklet XVI, 94–96.

58 Name withheld for privacy purposes.

59 Large amount of blood loss resulting in death.

Hoping for more, I waited.

"We, the Jury find that (a) the bullet which killed Maria Elizabeth Steinhauser came from the gun of a member of the tactical squad, their action was precipitated by inmate Andrew Bruce because he held Miss Steinhauser between himself and the tactical squad in a manner leading the tactical squad to believe that her life was immediate jeopardy [sic] from his knife. Although this attaches responsibility to both the tactical squad and Andrew Bruce, we find that the tactical squad was justified in their action inasmuch as they acted in the line of duty in the firm belief that they were acting to save Miss Steinhauser's life, that the irresponsible action of inmates Andrew Bruce, Dwight Lucas, and Claire Wilson in the taking of hostages led to the death of Maria Elizabeth Steinhauser.

"We, the Jury, recommend:

"(a) In any penitentiary hostage-taking incident, control over the entire action shall be vested in an outside body trained in the handling of such incidents. Such body to include personnel trained in liaison, communications, negotiations, and tactical operations. Such body shall have sufficient numbers to allow for sufficient rest periods. The Solicitor General shall be responsible for taking the initiative in forming such bodies.

"(2) It is recognized that an interim time lapse may occur before the arrival of the outside body, and a sufficiently trained staff should be available within the institution on the following basis: (a) For each shift, certain individuals (noncustodial) will be pretrained and designated as liaison officers (b) For each shift, certain individuals will be pretrained and designated as the interim tactical team.

"(3) That the local police, in whose jurisdiction the penitentiary lies, send a qualified investigative team, especially as to procedures of interrogation, to be within the penitentiary from the start of the incident to work in conjunction with the 'outside body' in control.

"(4) That the evidence presented during this Inquest points to the frustration and tension of inmates as to their future transfers or sentencing to 'S.C.U.' as being the main contributing factor precipitating this hostage-taking incident. The jury recommends that procedures be developed or an outside body be formed to better ensure that disciplinary action is fair.

"(5) That the classification building be under tighter security and inmates be screened before entry into same.

"Signed by Jury Members."

With that pronouncement, the coroner thanked the jury members for their service and dismissed them.

I was stunned. Incredulous. Was that all there was?

Was there no recommendation for a further exhaustive police inquiry, possibly by the RCMP, to satisfy our family's concerns that Mary's death was not simply happenstance? Was there to be no effort to determine the suitability of various members of the penitentiary staff to work in the penal system? Was there to be no slap on the wrist, no punishment, no consequence for the squad member who'd tampered with evidence? Was there to be no further inquiry into the actions of the New Westminster Police Department who failed to perform an adequate investigation? Would there be no recommendations for the training, educational, and empathic requirements for the correctional staff?

But it was over. It really was the end.

Picking up my belongings and bidding farewell to my loyal friend, I drifted outside into the warm summer night and headed up to catch the ferry to the Sunshine Coast for one last visit with my beloved parents before returning to Toronto.

20

SONG OF MARY

I sing a song of Mary.
Were you ever at her place
laughing with the earth?

Anticipation always rang
when Mary was about.

I light a flame for Mary.
Do you believe in dreams?
It was very easy,
when Mary was about.

Where have you gone?
Can you see me now?
And if you do
I hope I'm true
to living up to life
as if Mary was about.

—Penny G., roommate and friend

FORTY-FOUR YEARS HAVE PASSED SINCE I walked out of the coroner's court and into the warm July evening, still not quite believing what I'd just heard. Without doubt, those sixteen days of intensely painful testimonies were the some of the most difficult and heart-wrenching days of my life. I felt hollow.

So much had happened to assault my mind and spirit.

A few weeks passed as I tried to massage my feelings and recapture the remnants of my former self.

Then one morning I woke with a start. I would write Mary's story. I would bend my efforts to give life in print to the full magnificence of her life and the tragedy of her death.

It would be a lifelong pursuit.

Very soon after returning to Toronto that summer in 1976, I quit my teaching job, turning my back on my personal and professional life in that city and returned to BC to begin feverishly researching the background to the first chapters of Mary's story. With a proposed outline for her biography, I reached out to a number of Canadian publishers, one of whom offered me a contract and assigned me an editor. I began writing, and had completed several chapters when suddenly, out of the blue, life itself interrupted me.

I was pregnant!

Hardly believing my good fortune, I could think of nothing else. What a wonderful gift! Now the upcoming birth of my first child was all consuming. My energies and focus were diverted from my writing to the amazing reality of welcoming a new life into the world.

Knowing that it would be some years before I would resume writing, I carefully stored the drafts of the first few chapters in the bottom drawer of my file cabinet. There they lay, patiently waiting until I would pick them up again and begin writing anew.

Over four decades would pass.

Even though Mary's life ended on June 11, 1975, her story was alive and well.

The first indication that Mary's story was still fresh in the public domain came on July 13, 1976, when, more than one year after Mary's death, the *Tabling of the Farris Report*[60] in the Canadian House of Commons in Ottawa was announced by the solicitor general's department. In both English and French, the communiqué read, *"the release of the report had been first delayed when murder charges were preferred against two of the*

---

60 *Tabling of the Farris Report*, News release/communiqué, July 13, 1976, Department of the Solicitor General, Public Affairs: 992-6819; 992-0541.

hostage takers" and then *"delayed again until the completion of an inquest by Coroner Doug Jacks [sic] into the death of Mary Steinhauser."*

Reassuring the public of the government's firm grip on the situation, Commissioner Therrien was quick to point out that many of the recommendations of the Farris Commission had already been acted upon. Such procedures focused primarily, he said, on the movement of inmates and control and security of the institution, i.e., the creation of emergency response teams, better control of kitchen knives, the searching of inmates, control of inmate movement, and an alarm system installed in the classification building. In addition, Therrien asserted, a closer liaison had been *"developed with the Royal Canadian Mounted Police and local police forces with respect to assistance that may be required during similar incidents."*

Again, I felt deeply disappointed and frustrated at the lack of a deeper and more profound investigation into the wider issues that led to Mary's death.

Not long after, however, a second, very poignant reminder that Mary's story still resonated deeply with the public arose.

It was Christmas Day, 1976.

I was speeding east along Columbia Street in New Westminster in my blue Olds Cutlass. Now four months pregnant, I was on my way to the suburb of Delta for Christmas dinner with friends. As I drove east past the B.C. Penitentiary entrance on Columbia Street, I noticed a small cluster of people milling about in front of the gates at the foot of the concrete stairway which rose up to the imposing prison gatehouse on the hill above.

What caught my eye was the long banner the group was holding up for all passersby to see. In bold, black letters, it read:

Did Mary Steinhauser die in vain?

Shocked, yet deeply moved at the same time, I wondered, *Who are these people? Why are they raising Mary's name and her sacrifice so provocatively in front of the prison?*

But the traffic was hurtling along Columbia, and there was no place to pull over, so I couldn't stop to query anyone about why they were there. I had to keep driving. I was already late for a family gathering.

I never did find out who the group was but have since come to believe that they were probably members or sympathizers of the prisoners' rights movement active around that time. Why would they care about Mary? The answer was simple. Through her tireless work and advocacy, Mary was loved, admired, and respected by many of the B.C. Penitentiary and Matsqui inmates. She was their champion, and admired by all those who were deeply concerned with prisoners' rights, prison justice, and penal reform.

Five months after this incident, my first daughter, Louisa, was born. Without question, it was one of the happiest days of my life. I felt blessed and grateful for this wonderful gift. I threw myself into building a new life that centred on my precious little girl.

Two years passed before a third reminder that Mary's story still throbbed in the public imagination came knocking at my door.

His name was Christian Bruyère.[61] He was a playwright, he said, and wanted to write the story of the hostage-taking, which he hoped would form the script for a stage play. Would I talk to him and tell him about Mary? Cautiously I agreed to meet up with him, and over the following months I learned that he admired Mary's compassion and bravery. He soon completed the script for *Walls*,[62] and on May 5, 1978, I was at the opening night performance at the Vancouver East Cultural Centre in Vancouver, B.C. Directed by Jace van der Veen, *Walls* was promoted as a "documentary drama based on the hostage-taking at the B.C. Penitentiary, which resulted in the death of Mary Steinhauser." Mary was played by Susan Wright,[63] and Danny Baker (as Andrew Bruce) by Winston Rekert.[64]

I remember feeling as if the whole exercise was unreal, the actors went about their business but it seemed as if they were just acting. One distinct

---

61 Christian Bruyère (1944–), film producer and writer, founder of Mystique Films, Vancouver, B.C.

62 1984 Canadian drama film directed by Tom Shandel, based on the theatrical play by Christian Bruyère.

63 Susan Wright ((1947–1991), Canadian actress.

64 Winston Rekert (1949–2012), Gemini Award–winning Canadian actor, artist, producer, and director.

memory is that the casting of Susan Wright as Mary was disconcerting for me because Susan had blond hair and Mary had long black hair. The one standout performance was Winston Rekert as Danny Baker. He was menacing but believably vulnerable at the same time.

In that same year, more evidence of the staying power of Mary's story arose in the form of a young Vancouver singer/songwriter by the name of Bob Mercer[65] who was busy penning the lyrics "Wilson, Lucas and Bruce/ Everybody's Crazy But You and Me," a haunting ballad about the hostage-taking and Mary's death. At a recording session, Mercer and his band *The Explosions* (Jamie Baugh, Tom Harrison, Dave Lester, and Alex Varty) would produce a 45 rpm record, which remains today as a haunting and graphic recounting of the way Mary died and the price she paid for "the friends she made."

WILSON, LUCAS, AND BRUCE
By Bob Mercer

Do you remember on the ninth of June/
When it came on the radio
Or maybe you saw the headline/
Maybe you still don't know
It said: three cons have taken fifteen hostages/
Holding 'em there with a knife
Three men betting on freedom/Betting with the rest of their life
Do you remember a woman named Mary/
She was held on the edge of a blade
But she never died from no knife at her throat/
She died for the friends she made

Because a man or a woman in chains
They got to fight to keep from going insane
Wilson, Lucas, and Bruce
Crazy enough to cut themselves loose

---

65 Bob Mercer. Canadian musician, songwriter, and singer.

Call for the prison director/Someone's committed a crime
It's Andy Bruce, Dwight Lucas, and Clare Wilson, sir/
They're leaving before their time
Call the solicitor general/Wake up the chain of command
Cause Andy's got a knife at Mary's throat/
Just so we can understand his demand
To be flown to some other country/That won't put him down in a hole
Just got to go to some other place, Lord/
That don't got to control his very soul

Because a man or a woman in chains
They got to fight to keep from going insane
Wilson, Lucas, and Bruce
Crazy enough to cut themselves loose
Do you remember on June the eleventh/
Could you believe your ears
And do you remember how the truth trickled out/
Confirming the worst of your fears
Andy killed Mary, the prison guards said/
They had to shoot Andy Bruce in the head
While Andy lay bleeding and Mary lay dead/
Don't you remember the lies that they spread
But the truth will be known where people are free
And it's the only freedom in that penitentiary
And it grows like the echo of a steel door/
And it trickles like blood 'cross a cold stone floor
And it rose with the sun till they knew everyone/
That Mary had died from a prison guard's gun

Now the inquiry came and the inquiry went/Nobody heard the truth
A coroner's jury and later a trial/And still not a shred of the proof
Now what does it say about justice? What does it say for the law
And all of the lawyers, the cops, and politicians/
If nobody saw what that bleeding man saw
Or we lock up a man for a killing/Thank God for the government

> Then we strip down all hope but to break out or die/
> But when someone goes it's called an "accident"
> And the judges will say that the case is closed/
> But I just don't see how that can be
> The story ain't over till we tear down the walls/
> And all of God's children are free
> We gotta set them free/We gotta set them free
>
> Because a man or a woman in chains
> They got to fight to keep from going insane
> Wilson, Lucas, and Bruce
> Crazy enough to cut themselves loose
> They gonna cut themselves loose/They gonna cut themselves loose
>
> Because a man or a woman in chains
> They got to fight to keep from going insane
> Wilson, Lucas, and Bruce
> Crazy enough to cut themselves loose
> They gonna cut themselves loose/They gonna cut themselves loose

The year 1979 arrived and with it the birth of my second lovely baby girl, Erica, who brought a kind of peace and comfort to my heart. In a very tangible way, our two daughters brought our family great solace and hope for the future. Their sweetness and *joie de vivre* were antidotes to the pain and loss we all felt when Mary died.

I thought about Mary often. Always at Christmas, her birthday, and the anniversary of her death. But also oftentimes when I looked at my little girls; I grieved for their loss, because they would never know an aunt called Mary.

For the next five years, my life was governed and shaped by the immediate concerns and demands of raising my daughters while managing our household.

Then in 1984, once again Mary was in the spotlight, this time coming alive as a character in the movie *Walls*, based on the stage play by the same name, directed by Tom Shandel and produced by Christian Bruyère. In the film, Mary was played by Andrée Pelletier, a young French Canadian actor, while Andy Bruce was reprised by Winston Rekert.

In the fall of that year, an invitation arrived in my mailbox to attend the private screening of the film at the Studio Theatre on Granville Street in Vancouver on Friday, November 23. With some trepidation about what I was about to see, I went to the screening and saw for the second time my sister played by another woman. For some reason, the film version was more unsettling than the stage play had been. Mainly because Pelletier's performance failed to capture the essence of Mary's powerful persona and strength of character. It was a timid version of Mary, lacking in passion or veracity. Even more upsetting, however, was the powerful effect the final scene had on me, which was the shooting itself. I've only ever had the fortitude to watch the final scene in the film version of *Walls* twice in my life, because I simply could not bear to watch that final horrific scene.

Regrettably, the critical reviews of *Walls* were not kind. In his review, Peter Wilson of the *Sun* newspaper began[66] with the assertion that the "cause of prison reform will not be helped by *Walls*, a Vancouver-made feature film that fictionalizes the 1975 hostage-taking incident at the B.C. Penitentiary in New Westminster." It was, Wilson wrote, "so one-sided, so bleeding-hearted, so polemical…that it can only preach to the converted."

Wilson continued by first praising Rekert's performance of Danny Baker (aka Andy Bruce) as "a good one, full of anger and quickly changing moods" and then criticizing "Baker's actions and attitudes, because they dominate the film at the expense of the Tremblay's [aka Mary Steinhauser's] character." Wilson makes the case that the film should have been Tremblay's (Mary's) story but fails to do so "because she [Mary] is presented more as an attitude than as a human being." Instead, "the resulting domination by the Baker character of what should have been Tremblay's story unbalances the film."

In the years following the making of *Walls*, it was subsequently renamed as *Lockup* for an American audience and reappears from time to time on

---

66 [Peter] Wilson quoted from his review, "On One Side of Reality," *Vancouver Sun*, November 23, 1984.

movie channels as either *Walls* or *Lockup*. With all its flaws, *Walls* remains the only cinematic nod to that terrible event and Mary's tragic sacrifice.

It was now the late 1980s, and I was to suffer yet more devastating loss: both my mother and father died within a year of each other. At times after my parents' deaths, I felt very much alone…All of my family had now passed, and I was an orphan. I had no relatives except for my German cousins on my father's side, none of whom I'd ever met, and who all lived in Southern Germany.

My family responsibilities and my teaching positions kept me busy. My daughters were getting older and better able to care for themselves, so I went back into education, ending up teaching English Language classes in various private post-secondary institutions throughout the Lower Mainland.

In September 1995, I returned to my old alma mater, Simon Fraser University to begin my program of studies for a MEd degree in Curriculum and Instruction.

Five years later, I proudly marched across the stage in the SFU main concourse to accept my degree. Looking on were my now-adult daughters, who surprised me with a huge bouquet of spring flowers and cheered me on as I walked across the stage. Their presence there was very important to me, and I was so charged with gratitude and love for the two young women who, in time, would go on to build their own lives and legacies. For the moment, my energies were directed to getting and keeping a well-paying job to secure my future.

Taking a backseat to my pressing domestic concerns, Mary's story would have to wait for a few years yet.

Then one Sunday afternoon in November 2003, almost three decades after Mary's death, I was out and about in my community and picked up a copy of the *Province* newspaper. Flipping through the pages, a big black bold headline leapt out at me.

Margaret Franz

Who killed Mary Steinhauser?[67]

There was no love lost between the prison social workers, of whom she was one, and the guards who shot her during a hostage-taking. Now a former paramedic who was at the scene says she was shot on purpose.

I was shocked. Shot on purpose? A new investigation? How could this be?

Above the provocative headline was a 1975 *Province* archival photo showing the inner courtyard of the B.C. Penitentiary and the classification building with the attached vault. Below the headline was a headshot of a bespectacled man with the caption, "*George High says a guard said: 'Kill her, kill her.'*"

I read on.

"*The New Westminster police have launched an investigation into the death of Mary Steinhauser, shot by prison guards in the old B.C. Penitentiary,*" the story began. "*This new investigation came following the accusation of a former ambulance medic, George High, who a month before, made a videotaped statement to police saying he overheard a guard say, 'Kill her, kill her,' before the rescue attempt.*"

Apparently Mr. High was convinced that at least one guard intended to shoot Steinhauser. "*There's no question in my mind that Mary Steinhauser was purposefully shot,*" he said.

Recalling those final moments, High said that he was in a nearby trailer with one other paramedic and several tense guards when a man wearing street clothes burst in yelling, "*It's going down! Go! Go! Go!*"

High's partner was on a mobile telephone requesting backup as High and the guards left the trailer for the hostages' vault. "*There is no question in my mind, I heard somebody saying, 'Kill her, kill her.' It was said very loudly, very distinctly,*" High said.

As High entered the room, "*There was a melee going on, people fighting and shouting.*" High, lying on his stomach, helped another man drag a wounded woman into the hallway.

---

67   Steve Berry, "Who Killed Mary Steinhauser?" *Province*, November 2, 2003.

The injured woman was Mary Steinhauser. She was not breathing, he said. She did not have a pulse. High accompanied her to hospital, where he began emergency treatment until an intern arrived, although *"everybody knew it was a lost cause."*

High was surprised that he wasn't called to testify at the Farris Commission Inquiry. None of the medics were called to testify. High admitted he spent little time with the guards but mentioned that *"It was well known they disliked social workers in general, and Steinhauser specifically. Other paramedics who were in close contact with the guards for several days backed High's contention that the guards disliked social workers.*

"'The guards felt that the prison classification staff were sympathetic to the inmates,' said 30-year veteran paramedic Bruce Brink, who spent a number of shifts in the trailer. 'My betting is that she [Mary] was in the way.'"

When told of High's charges, the prison officials said they would wait for a police investigation before acting. But they had no plans to reopen any investigation unless the police "decided to look into the matter, at which point they would co-operate fully with them," said Dennis Findlay, a spokesman for the Correctional Service of Canada.

But why had High waited so long before coming forward with his suspicions? the author asked.

At first, High explained, he expected to be called to the inquiry, but wasn't. Then he was reluctant to speak out publicly because, as a government employee, he was effectively gagged. *"I've had to hold my tongue all these years,"* he said.

"High was diagnosed with accumulative stress disorder in 1998."

I put down the newspaper but picked it up later and read it over and over.

What should I do? What could I do?

Some days later, I arrived at the New Westminster Police Department and asked to speak to the investigating officer. I can't remember exactly what the officer said, but I distinctly recall my feeling that, to this man, Mary's story seemed to be a cold case.

A very cold case.

He mentioned that they would wait for more evidence or statements from the public. He would keep me informed, he said, of any new developments.

I waited patiently for some kind of response, but none came.

I wondered if the police ever questioned all six members of the tactical squad about High's statement. And the two other medics? Or possibly other witnesses out in the community? Perhaps they had. In any case, I didn't hear anything. It was quietly dropped.

After all, it was a very cold case.

In the first decade of the twenty-first century, Mary's name took pride of place on two official Canadian historical monuments three thousand miles apart. Because she was both a federal and a provincial employee at the time of her death, her name appears on the glass panel monument at the Canadian Police and Peace Officers' Memorial on Capitol Hill in Ottawa, Ontario, and on the Bastion,[68] a sixty-thousand-pound granite monument just behind the Parliament Buildings in Victoria, the seat of the Provincial Government of British Columbia. The Bastion is a four-sided memorial with eight separate panels representing different aspects of the peace officer community in B.C. Eight "Fallen Hero panels" are on the exterior corners of the monument, with names appearing in random order. Interestingly, the name recorded on one of the eight panels for my sister was her birth name, Maria Elizabeth Steinhauser, even though for all her childhood and adult years, she was always known as "Mary".

It was now the second decade of the new millennium, and for a few years I'd been toying with the idea of establishing an educational bursary in Mary's name. It would be a bursary for Aboriginal students in Arts and Social Sciences, with a preference for those studying criminology. This seemed fitting because Mary was an confirmed believer in education as transformative and because, at the time she died, she was intending to return to SFU to study for her PhD in Criminology. Simon Fraser University was the logical choice. It was, after all, where Mary and me both

---

68 Walking tour pamphlet, "Outdoor Self-Guided Walking Tour" produced by the Legislative Assembly of British Columbia, *Leg.bc.ca/content-peo/Documents/Legislative-Assembly-Walking-Tour-English.pdf*.

studied in the late '60s and acquired our undergraduate degrees at roughly the same time.

I knew that Mary would be proud to have a bursary named after her which would support Aboriginal students and be based on need alone. This last point was very important since Mary herself worked so hard at various jobs to support herself financially throughout her university years for the sole purpose of avoiding the mountain of debt so often incurred by post-secondary students. At a deeply personal level, she understood what bursaries and other financial awards meant to struggling students.

In 2011, I established the Mary Steinhauser Memorial Bursary for SFU Aboriginal Undergraduate Students in Arts and Social Sciences. In the next calendar year, the bursary paid out its first award to a hardworking and dedicated Indigenous woman in the Faculty of Education who was, coincidentally, a single mother studying to be a teacher. What a perfect fit, and exactly the type of student Mary would identify with and be proud to support!

Only a year later, a beautifully written and evocative article entitled "Mary's Song," by Ron Verzuh was published in the November 2012 edition of *aq Magazine*,[69] a publication for SFU alumni. For many of the alumni who read this article, it was "new" news. Since many hadn't been around in 1975, they were completely unfamiliar with her story.

Following close on the publication of the *aq* story came my theatre performance project to fundraise for Mary's bursary. Entitled *BRAVE: the Mary Steinhauser Legacy*, this performance would tell the story of Mary's entire life, not just the day she died or the way she died. This *"Evening of Story, Song and Dance"* would *"celebrate Mary's inspired life as a nurse, social, worker, Canadian peace officer, and passionate advocate or prison reform."* Proceeds from the ticket sales would go towards funding Mary's bursary.

Planning for the *BRAVE* event took almost eighteen months and involved many talented and dedicated friends, actors, and interested parties, who volunteered their time and energy to pull it all together. It was a massive effort.

On the day of the performance, several historical displays were set up in the lobby of the Terry Fox Theatre in Port Coquitlam. These displays were

---

69   no longer in publication

all related in some way to different stages of Mary's life and place of work. The window display featured various mannequins, one of Mary dressed in period-specific uniforms first as a student psychiatric nurse, another of Mary as a graduate nurse, and a third as Mary in civilian clothes as she would have worn as a classification officer at the B.C. Penitentiary. All the displays including several male mannequins, one as an inmate and another as a prison guard. The mannequins were dressed, mounted, and curated by Anna Tremere of the once-active Riverview Hospital Historical Society and her volunteer assistants. The New Westminster Museum curator and the Thompson Rivers University Archives Department representatives were also present, bringing displays of artifacts and memorabilia related to the B.C. Penitentiary and the Mary Steinhauser Display at the Kamloops Courthouse, Kamloops, B.C.

Finally, it was Showtime! On Saturday, March 29, 2014, *BRAVE: the Mary Steinhauser Legacy* came alive onstage in front of an appreciative and mesmerized audience of 220 people.

It was an awe-inspiring performance.

Not only was it a magnificent success creatively imagined by Karen Freeborn, the director, and Ross Friesen, the technical director, but the performance also featured both real-life characters playing themselves and actors portraying various people in Mary's life.

We raised almost $7,000 that night.

Only a year later, still buoyed and encouraged by the success of *BRAVE*, I decided to retire from my university teaching position at Kwantlen Polytechnic University in Surrey, B.C., to take up writing Mary's story once again.

But first I had to do something very important. I had to locate the record of the witness testimony of the 1976 B.C. coroner's inquest into Mary's death.

Why did I need it? Primarily to help me recall the details of some of the crucial stories of several of those twenty-nine witnesses who testified at the inquest over those six weeks in 1976.

Somewhere, deep in the bowels of a provincial government storage facility, this record existed.

It knew it was there somewhere. It had to be. After all, hadn't the inquest been the longest-running inquest in B.C.'s history? But where? Forty-three years had passed. Would anyone be able to find these records? Would they still exist? Perhaps they'd all be destroyed by now.

I began my search.

Several months of emails and phone calls followed.

While waiting for a response, I decided to host another fundraiser for Mary's bursary. I planned a forum to take place during Mental Health Week in May 2018, to encourage discussion around mental health. Forming the panel at this forum were two knowledgeable mental health experts in the community. The first presenter was Anna Tremere, former curator of the Riverview Hospital museum, provided a history lesson about the once grand and sprawling mental health facility in Coquitlam, B.C., now largely shuttered and abandoned. The second presenter was Dr John Higenbottam who spoke to the ensuing lack of mental health resources in the region while providing a blueprint for his vision of a brand new community mental health centre focusing on training, education, and housing. Rounding out the panel was Jennifer Coutu, a young, bright, articulate SFU Indigenous student, who described her life and experiences as an out-of-town student, financially strapped and depending on bursaries and scholarships to fund her education.

In my welcome address, I spoke about how mental health was one of Mary's key concerns when it came to her inmate clients at Matsqui Institution and the B.C. Penitentiary back in the mid-'70s. At that critical juncture in her career, she understood how deeply mental illness in all its variant forms saturated criminality and all things related to incarceration. The existence of drug dependency among inmates was well known. What was lesser well-known was how solitary confinement units were often used to manage inmate behaviour, sometimes with unexpected and tragic consequences.

It was during her time at the B.C. Penitentiary that Mary met with Don Sorochan, QC, a young Vancouver lawyer who, along with his senior partner, Bryan Williams, QC, was moving ahead with efforts to bring organized challenges to the solitary confinement of B.C. Pen prisoners. The lawyers had agreed to act as counsel in the case of McCann v. The Queen.[70]

In his submission to my book, Sorochan[71] writes about the circumstances that brought him into contact with Mary.

Arrangements were made with the director of the British Columbia penitentiary, Dragan Cernetic, for me to interview every prisoner confined in the special correctional unit. These included prisoners held in protective custody and pursuant to sentences from the institution "warden courts" as well as "administrative segregation."

> *My first dealings with Mary came as a result of me interviewing a severely mentally ill prisoner. I had several interviews with this prisoner because I required assistance in communicating with him, since he was a French Canadian with very limited English language ability. The prisoner was clearly schizophrenic and floridly psychotic. Other than his mental illness, however, there did not appear to be any basis justifying his detention in solitary confinement. Mary had responsibilities as the prisoner's Classification Officer, so I approached her to see if something could be done about removing this prisoner from segregation and having him transferred to the recently established Regional Psychiatric Centre (a penitentiary in Matsqui).*
>
> *My meetings with Mary about this were memorable. At the first meeting she showed a great deal of compassion about the circumstances of this prisoner, and shared my desire to have him transferred to the Regional Psychiatric Centre. I seem to recall that she had a background dealing with the mentally ill and understood how this psychosis could be treated. However, the prisoner committed suicide*

---

70   For details see Professor Michael Jackson's book, *Justice Behind the Walls*, at http://www.justicebehindthewalls.net/book.asp?cid=760.

71   Private correspondence containing written responses to interview questions about Mr. Sorochan's meetings with Mary between 1973–1975 regarding solitary confinement issues at the B.C. Penitentiary.

by garroting himself with his bed sheets. I met again with Mary after the suicide. She was very upset, particularly at the attitude of those running the Regional Psychiatric Centre. They refused the prisoner's transfer on the basis that he was "too crazy" and would disrupt their group programs. I tried to raise the issues related to this man's death at an inquest, but the inquest was held without giving me the requested notice, and with no discussion of any institutional issues relating to the death.

The tragedy of this inmate's death in a solitary confinement cell struck a painful chord in me, because once again I was reminded of the reason why the three inmates had taken Mary and the other fifteen prison personnel hostage. Andy Bruce's words haunted me.[72] *"I would rather have been killed outright you know. At least you'd die with a little dignity, you know, not the way them people die up there [SCU]."*

Not only that, but Sorochan's story illustrated the cruelty of solitary confinement itself. It brought into sharp focus the fatal consequences of bureaucratic indifference that would deny a very sick man treatment in a psychiatric hospital built especially for such inmates. On a personal level, it spoke to Mary's keen understanding and awareness of the nature of this man's illness and where he ought to be housed and treated, with dignity and respect. And finally, it spoke to her righteous indignation at the penitentiary administrators, who would turn their back on a desperate man, ultimately resulting in his death by his own hand.

What helpless rage Mary must have felt!

Summer came and went, and I'd almost lost hope of hearing about the inquest documents. But in November 2018, the good news came.

Miraculously, the entire coroner's transcript of record was found! There they lay, untouched and forgotten for forty-two years, deep in the bowels of the B.C. Coroner Service's vault, the entire transcript of record of the Inquest on the Death of Maria Elizabeth Steinhauser. In all, there were

---

72 An alternate term for solitary confinement unit.

2,237 pages bound in sixteen discreet booklets—one booklet for each day of the sixteen days of riveting testimony by twenty-nine witnesses.

And it all came about because, in response to my plea, a determined young female Coroners Service employee, with the support and encouragement of her manager and her co-worker, took the time and made the extra effort to locate the box of sixteen booklets. I was so grateful and ecstatic, all at the same time!

So it was that in February 2019, I promised myself that I would make the main focus of my life the completion of Mary's story, and furthermore, I would not rest until it was complete.

I began to write in earnest.

I was making progress with my writing when two events occurred which, once again, reminded me that the story of Mary's life was far from over…The first event was the endowment of the Mary Steinhauser Memorial Bursary for SFU Aboriginal Undergraduate Students in Arts and Social Sciences. After fundraising for eight long years, I'd finally reached the $20,000 mark for this namesake bursary for my sister. At this point, an annual award would be paid out in perpetuity to an SFU Aboriginal undergraduate student, based on the interest on the principal alone. Although donations could still be made to the bursary, there was no need for me to continue to fundraise. The fund was now self-generating.

The second happening was a monumental tribute to the strength and power of Mary's story. For a few years, I'd been searching for a permanent home for my papers and memorabilia regarding Mary. At some point, I approached the Simon Fraser University Library and asked if they'd be interested in housing such a collection. Very quickly, after learning about Mary, the head of Special Collections and Rare Books, Melissa Salrin, examined my materials and agreed that Mary would be commemorated in a signature collection, the Mary Steinhauser Research Collection in the Simon Fraser University Library's Special Collections and Rare Books Division at the main campus on Burnaby Mountain.

What a rare, yet exquisitely deserving honour for Mary! I was delighted at the public recognition of how important Mary's story and life is.

When this book is published, the SFU library will be the recipient of my large collection of papers, articles and memorabilia about Mary and they, in turn, will collect, catalogue, and make the Mary Steinhauser Research Collection available to a global audience of academics, researchers, and interested members of the public.

And finally, this book will be a part of the collection.

I had one final question: Did Mary die in vain?

The answer, of course, is "No."

Mary is a hero. She is a hero because at fifteen years of age, she saved the life of our eleven-year-old childhood friend from drowning.

She is a hero because she gave voice to, and acted upon, her beliefs that every life is worth saving.

She is a hero because she offered herself as the principal hostage during the forty-one-hour hostage-taking, acting as a human shield for one of the inmate hostage-takers.

She is a hero because, by her selfless act, she deflected the attention of the inmate hostage-takers away from the other fourteen hostages sequestered in the vault.

But most of all, Mary is a hero because she is a shining example of the light one person can bring to a dark and often brutal world.

Her voice will be heard.

Her story will go on.

"Gunfire kills woman hostage" *Vancouver Sun*, June 11, 1975.
Material republished with the express permission of Vancouver Sun, a division of Postmedia Network Inc.

"Six women carry Mary to her grave," *Province*, June 17, 1975.
Photo caption: Pallbearers carry the coffin of Mary Steinhauser past an honour guard of more than 50 policemen and prison guards.
Material republished with the express permission of Vancouver Province, a division of Postmedia Network Inc.

Picture 1: Honour Guard flanks cortège exiting from Blessed Sacrament Church, June 17, 1975. Picture 2: Mary's gravestone, Forest Lawn Cemetery, Burnaby, B.C.

"A FAMILY'S GRIEF is shared by Mr. and Mrs. August Steinhauser and their daughter Margaret Rose, as they attend burial service for their daughter Mary, who died during clash between inmates and guards at B.C. Penitentiary," *Vancouver Sun*, June 17, 1975.

"Inmate names guard in Steinhauser death: Pen shooting details submitted to court," *Vancouver Sun*, January 21, 1976. Material republished with the express permission of Vancouver Sun, a division of Postmedia Network Inc.

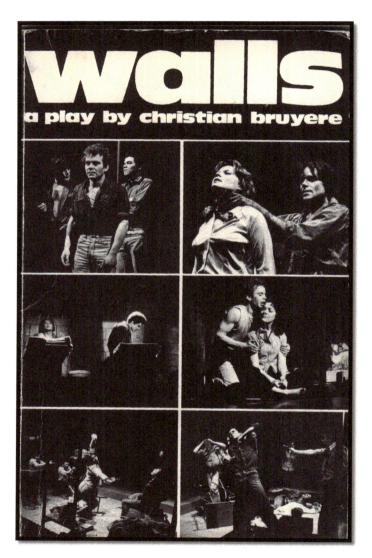

Walls, a play by Christian Bruyère, Talonbooks 1978.

Front page of jacket: *Wilson, Lucas & Bruce: Everybody's Crazy But You & Me*, by Bob Mercer, singer/songwriter and the Explosions

"Who killed Mary Steinhauser?" by Steve Berry, *Province*, November 2, 2003.

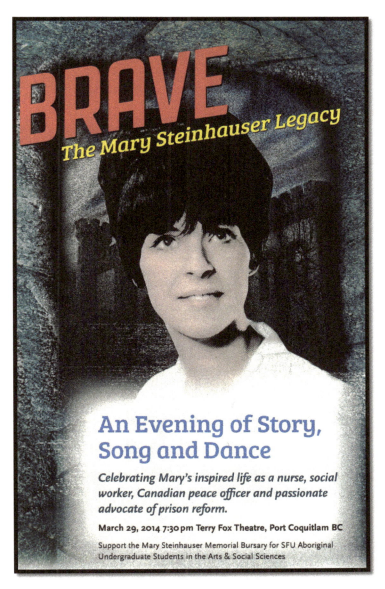

Image 1: Cover, Design: Jane Edwards Griffin, Griffin Design, TriCity Printing. Program for *BRAVE: The Mary Steinhauser Legacy*, theatre production. An Evening of Story, Song and Dance, March 29, 2014, 7:30 p.m., Terry Fox Theatre, Port Coquitlam, B.C.

BRAVE
The Mary Steinhauser Legacy

PRODUCED BY MARGARET FRANZ | DIRECTED BY KAREN FREEBORN

PROGRAM

Welcome Song – Ama litwxsim (Standfast)	Dancers of Damelahamid
Greetings & Opening Remarks	Margaret Franz
A Daring Rescue	written by Margaret Franz and presented by Elizabeth Elwood
June's Memories	written by Margaret Franz and presented by Baiba Thomson
I Car-Pooled with Mary	written and presented by Mae Burrows
Wilson, Lucas and Bruce	written & performed by Bob Mercer
Ten-Year Stretch	from writings of an ex-inmate (anonymous) presented by Tom Little
Convicts Lose a Friend	written & performed by Dennis Neveu
Mary was my Angel	from writings of an ex-inmate (anonymous) presented by Brad Nickason
Song of Mary	written by Petra Graves and voiced-over by Carly Friesen
The Mary Steinhauser Memorial Bursary	Margaret Franz
Video of Nancy Johnson	2012 MSMB Recipient
Presentation to Janelle Kasperski	2014 MSMB Recipient
Song – Bekxw 'nuum (All that we are)	Dancers of Damelahamid
Final Remarks	Karen Freeborn

TECHNICAL
Visual Compilation and Video-Taping by Ross Friesen

PRODUCER'S NOTE

As her younger sister, it's been my goal for almost 40 years to tell the remarkable story of Mary's inspired life as a nurse, social worker and Canadian peace officer while continuing her legacy of bravery, compassion, and advocacy of social justice through the bursary established in her name. With the generous help of so many who shared my vision, this night is the culmination of that dream. I thank you so much for being here.
– MARGARET FRANZ
Founder of Mary Steinhauser Memorial Bursary for SFU Aboriginal Undergraduate Students in Arts & Social Sciences

DIRECTOR'S NOTE

Twelve years ago, the story of Mary Steinhauser was told to me by an inmate who had lived the effects of Mary's compassion and unyielding dedication. Through his eyes, I witnessed Mary's bravery as she forged ahead to incorporate a new model of rehabilitation in the Penitentiary system. I felt the power of her brave resolve to fight for social justice and human rights within this new model, and against fierce opposition. I observed, through this man, the great love and respect that he and so many other inmates had for Mary, in an era when incarceration was synonymous with severe and unusual punishment; and I felt the sting of tears the inmates shed when they lost her. It is for this reason that I am honoured to be a part of **BRAVE** –The Mary Steinhauser Legacy.

We endeavor this evening to present Mary through the words of the people who knew and loved her. Their words make up this evening's presentation and provide a glimpse into Mary's spirit, strength and bravery.

I sincerely hope that Mary's story speaks to you, as it has spoken to me. Very best regards and enjoy the evening.
– KAREN FREEBORN

ROSS FRIESEN – *Technical Director*
Ross first became aware of Mary's story in June of last year and is pleased to be able to use his creative skills to contribute to **BRAVE** and to continue Mary's legacy.

Image 2: Inside pages 1 and 2: program and bios.

Left to right: Mannequins dressed in period costumes for (i) Mary as a student nurse at Essondale Hospital, (ii) Mary as a graduate nurse, and (iii) Mary as a classification officer at the B.C. Penitentiary. Lobby display, *BRAVE: The Mary Steinhauser Legacy* theatre performance, Terry Fox Theatre, Port Coquitlam, March 29, 2014, prepared by Anna Tremere, of former Riverview Hospital Historical Society. Photo Credit: Anna Tremere

Margaret Franz, Mary Steinhauser's sister, selected to lay the wreath for all the Families of the Fallen at the 2012 B.C. Police and Peace Officer's Memorial Ceremony in Stanley Park, September 30, 2012.
Photo Credit: Erik Tofsrud, Lost Lagoon Photos Inc.

August 1973: Mary comes to visit me in Toronto and we celebrate her birthday.

BIBLIOGRAPHY

"3 inmates swear Mary died protecting Bruce." Vancouver, B.C.: *Vancouver Sun*, June 27, 1975.

"Additional charges expected through Steinhauser inquest." Vancouver, B.C.: n.p., ca. 1976.

Allman, Warren. *Report of the Commission of Inquiry into Events at the British Columbia Penitentiary June 9 to 11, 1975*. Ottawa: Public Affairs Division of the Canadian Penitentiary Service and the National Parole Service. 1976. Accessed May 12, 2020. https://www.ncjrs.gov/pdffiles1/Digitization/47300NCJRS.pdf.

BC Booklook. "#82 Helen Potrebenko." B.C. author database. January 26, 2016. https://bcbooklook.com/2016/01/26/82-helen-potrebenko/.

"BC Pen hostages face death threat." Vancouver, B.C.: *Province*, June 10, 1975.

Berry, Steve. "Who killed Mary Steinhauser?" Vancouver, B.C.: *Province*, November 2, 2003.

Bird, Chris. "Different end if hostages had known?" Vancouver, B.C.: *Province*, June 27, 1975.

—"Mary yelled 'don't shoot,' prisoners say in affidavit." Vancouver, B.C.: *Province*, June 17, 1975.

—"Negotiators testify at B.C. Pen inquiry." Vancouver, B.C.: *Province*, June 27, 1975.

Bruyère, Christian. *Walls*. Vancouver, B.C.: Talonbooks, 1978.

Clark, Robert. *Down Inside: Thirty Years in Canada's Prison Service*. Fredericton, N.B.: Goose Lane Editions, 2017.

Coull, Gary. "15 hostages at knifepoint as lifers demand freedom." Vancouver,

B.C.: *Province*, June 10, 1975.

—"3rd time hostages taken." Vancouver, B.C.: *Province*, June 10, 1975.

—"Two ways to go—out of the country or end up dead." Vancouver, B.C.: *Province*, June 10, 1975.

Eberts, Tony. "Convicts lose a friend." Vancouver, B.C.: *Province*, June 12, 1975.

—"Victim dedicated life to helping desperate." Southam News Services, n.p., n.d.

Gray, Malcolm. "Prisoner-aid group charges that guard fired unnecessarily." Toronto, Ont.: *Globe and Mail*, June 27, 1975.

—"Handling of B.C. prison siege had aura of a war operation." Toronto, Ont.: *Globe and Mail*, June 20, 1975.

—"Questions unanswered as B.C. prison inquiry winds up its hearings." Toronto, Ont.: *Globe and Mail*, July 29, 1975.

Hall, Neal. "Closure of Riverview Hospital marks end of era in mental health treatment." *Vancouver Sun*, July 20, 2012. http://www.vancouversun.com/health/closure+riverview+hospital+marks+mental+health+treatment/6967310/story.html.

Harrison, Tom. "Remembering Mary Steinhauser." Vancouver, B.C.: Province, December 6, 2013. http://pressreader.com/Canada/the_province/20131206/282325382774229

Hendrickson, Bob. "Hostage tells her story of life and death in the vault." Vancouver, B.C.: *Province*, June 12, 1975.

Hills, Nick. "Doubt growing over secret B.C. Pen Inquiry." Vancouver, B.C.: *Province*, July 21, 1975.

Hoever, Hugo H., ed., *Saint Joseph Daily Missal*, New York: Catholic Book Publishing, 1961.

Hunter, Don. "Secrecy cloaks prison; hostage shot to death." Vancouver, B.C.: *Province*, June 12, 1975.

—"Six women carry Mary to her grave." Vancouver, B.C.: *Province*, June 17, 1975.

—"Inquest opens into death of Mary Steinhauser." Vancouver, B.C.: *Vancouver Sun*, May 26, 1976.

Jack, Doug. *Proceedings of the Inquest on the Death of Maria Elizabeth Stein-*

hauser. Witness Testimony Booklets I–XVI. New Westminster, B.C.: May 16, 1977.

Jackson, Michael. *Justice Behind the Walls: Human Rights in Canadian Prisons.* Vancouver, B.C.: Douglas and McIntyre, 2002. http://resolve.library.ubc.ca/cgi-bin/catsearch?bid=2553949.

Keats, Jordan. "History of Tranquille." Blog essay. http://blog.jordankeats.com/history-of-tranquille/.

Kelley, William R. "Why did the prisoners try to run?" Vancouver, B.C.: *Vancouver Sun*, June 17, 1975.

MacGuigan, Mark. *Report to Parliament of the Sub-Committee on the Penitentiary System in Canada.* Ottawa, Ont.: Minister of Supply and Services, 1977. Accessed May 12, 2020. https://johnhoward.ca/wp-content/uploads/2016/12/1977-HV-9507-C33-1977-MacGuigan.pdf.

MacLean, Neil B. *Serving Life 25: One Guard's Story.* Victoria, B.C.: Tellwell Talent, 2017.

Moersch, June E. "Did Mary Steinhauser die in vain?" Letter to the editor. Vancouver, B.C.: *Vancouver Sun*, February 3, 1976.

Moreau, Jennifer. "Meet Mae: she challenges the status quo." *Burnaby Now*, June 14, 2013. https://www.burnabynow.com/news/meet-mae-she-challenges-the-status-quo-1.407865.

"Murder charges stayed against B.C. Pen three." Newspaper article, n.p., n.d.

Murphy, P. J., ed. *The Anthony Martin BC Penitentiary Collection at the Old Courthouse,*

Kamloops, BC. An Old Courthouse/John Howard Society Publication. Kamloops, B.C.: Thompson Rivers University, 2012.

"No restrictions placed on B.C. Pen probe." Vancouver, B.C.: *Vancouver Sun*, June 16, 1975.

Odum, Jes and Larry Still. "Details of Mary's death still kept secret." Vancouver, B.C.: *Vancouver Sun*, June 25, 1975.

—"'Hit it! Hit it!' Pen Squad told." Vancouver, B.C.: *Vancouver Sun*, June 26, 1975.

—"Hostage tells of abuse at hands of knife-holding prison inmates." Vancouver, B.C.: *Vancouver Sun*, June 24, 1975.

—"'You'll dance now,' penitentiary man told." Vancouver, B.C.: *Vancouver Sun*, June 26, 1975.

Outdoor Self-Guided Walking Tour. Victoria, B.C.: Legislative Assembly of British Columbia, April 2018. Leg.bc.ca/content-peo/Documents/Legislative-Assembly-Walking-Tour-English.pdf.

Philcox, Pat, ed. *Whistle Stops Along the Columbia River Narrows: A History of Burton and Surrounding Area*. Burton New Horizons Book Committee. Manitoba: Friesen Printers, 1982.

"Police probe ownership of gun that killed Mary." Vancouver, B.C.: *Vancouver Sun*, July 5, 1975.

Poulsen, Chuck. "Guard named in prison shooting." Vancouver, B.C.: *Province*, January 21, 1976.

—"Mary made dying statement, court told." Vancouver, B.C.: *Province*, n.d.

Rowe, Peter. "Strange allies." *The Canadian*. Toronto, Ont.: Southstar Publishers Limited, May 28, 1977. ISSN: 0319-5139.

Spears, James. "Lucas Recounts last 10 seconds of Mary's life." Vancouver, B.C.: *Province*, June 23, 1976.

Spears, James and Alex Young. "Mystery surrounds fatal bullet." Vancouver, B.C.: *Vancouver Sun*, July 25, 1975.

Spears, Jim. "Beyond all our control." Vancouver, B.C.: *Province*, June 12, 1975.

—"Identity of Steinhauser killer still unknown." Vancouver, B.C.: *Province*, June 4, 1976.

St. Onge, David. *One Day…Gone*. Kingston, Ont.: Correctional Service Canada, 2014.

Steinhauser, Mary. "Single professional women in retirement." Master's thesis, School of Social Work, University of British Columbia, 1973. http://resolve.library.ubc.ca/cgi-bin/catsearch?bid=1560712.

Still, Larry. "Mary's slayer 'will remain a mystery forever.'" Vancouver, B.C.: *Vancouver Sun*, July 25, 1975.

—"Inmate names guard in Steinhauser death." Vancouver, B.C.: *Vancouver Sun*, January 21, 1976.

—"Pen siege guns 'not dusted for fingerprints.'" Vancouver, B.C.: *Vancouver Sun*, June 4, 1976.

—"Raiding penitentiary guards 'to disclose all.'" Vancouver, B.C.: *Vancouver Sun*, June 8, 1976.

—"The B.C. Pen case: one reporter's verdict." Vancouver, B.C.: *Vancouver Sun*, July 8, 1976.

Tabling of the Farris Report. News release. Ottawa, Ont.: Department of the Solicitor General, Public Affairs, July 13, 1976. 992-6819; 992-0541.

"Tear down the walls!" Castlegar, B.C.: *Arrow*, 2, no. 1 (Spring 1976).

Timson, Judith. "Prison siege victim buried." Toronto, Ont.: *Toronto Star*, June 17, 1975.

—"Steinhauser: Was she killed by B.C.'s jail system?" Toronto, Ont.: *Toronto Star*, January 26, 1976.

Tranquille Sanatorium Collection. Kamloops Museum and Archives. Compiled by Robb Gilbert, 2013. Revised July 2014. Revised January 2018 by Jaimie Fedorak. https://www.kamloops.ca/sites/default/files/docs/parks-recreation/tranquillesanatorium.pdf.

Verzuh, Ron. "Mary's Song." *aq Magazine*. Simon Fraser University, November 2012. https://www.sfu.ca/aq/issues/november2012/features/marys-song.html.

Young, Alex. "Solitary confinement 'inhumane'—Farris." Vancouver, B.C.: *Vancouver Sun*, July 4, 1975.

—"Deliberate Pen coverup charged." Vancouver, B.C.: *Province*, July 26, 1975.

—"Mary started to cry just before breakout." n.p., n.d.

—"Mary Steinhauser's sister wants justice done." Vancouver, B.C.: *Vancouver Sun*, May 27, 1976.

Young, Alex and Don Hunter. "Hostage sure some of them would die." Vancouver, B.C.: *Province*, June 24, 1975.

Wasserman, Jack. "Insider's outlook." Vancouver, B.C.: *Vancouver Sun*, June 26, 1975.

Wedman, Les. "Who will be the actress to play Mary Steinhauser?" Toronto, Ont.: n.p, n.d.

Wilson, Peter. "On One Side of Reality." Vancouver, B.C.: *Vancouver Sun*, November 23, 1984.

Wikipedia. *Mary Steinhauser.* https://en.wikipedia.org/wiki/Mary_Steinhauser. Links on the *Mary Steinhauser* page to the following entries:

—"Hostage dies as prison guards recapture 3 Canadian inmates." *New York Times*, June 12, 1975. https://web.archive.org/web/20110723023201/http:/bannerline.net/wiki_refs/times-stein.p. Retrieved November 22, 2014.

—"Knife at throat." *Ottawa Citizen*, February 20, 1976. https://news.google.com/newspapers?nid=2194&dat=19760220&id=EWk1AAAAIBAJ&sjid=rO0FAAAAIBAJ&pg=1057,1884833. Retrieved November 14, 2014.

—"One dies; siege ends." *Sarasota Journal*, June 11, 1975. https://news.google.com/newspapers?nid=1798&dat=19750611&id=AQ0fAAAAIBAJ&sjid=VI0EAAAAIBAJ&pg=5564,2114901. Retrieved November 14, 2014.

—"Penitentiary case: murder accused wants guard tried." *Ottawa Citizen*, August 19, 1975. https://news.google.com/newspapers?nid=2194&dat=19750819&id=naIyAAAAIBAJ&sjid=ku0FAAAAIBAJ&pg=891,714063. Retrieved November 14, 2014.

—"Victim had planned to quit prison job." *Eugene Register-Guard*, June 17, 1975. https://news.google.com/newspapers?nid=1310&dat=19750617&id=SLBEAAAAIBAJ&sjid=l9kDAAAAIBAJ&pg=6716,4357628. Retrieved November 14, 2014.

—"Woman hostage killed as jail siege ends." *Daily Telegraph*, June 12, 1975. https://web.archive.org/web/20110723023152/http:/bannerline.net/wiki_refs/telegraph-stein.pdf. Retrieved November 22, 2014.

—*Matsqui Institution.* https://en.wikipedia.org/wiki/Matsqui_Institution.

—*Riverview Hospital (Coquitlam).* https://en.wikipedia.org/wiki/Riverview_Hospital_(Coquitlam).

ACKNOWLEDGEMENTS

WRITING MARY'S STORY HAS BEEN a lifelong project. From beginning to end, many people have contributed their stories, their feelings, their insight, their memories of my sister, and their professional services to create an homage to both the magnificence of Mary's life and the tragedy of her death.

For those who contributed to the content of my book, I offer my most sincere and grateful thanks. They are, in order of appearance in Mary's story: Amy Doughty, the late June (Layton) Moersch, Sandra (Kendall) Girling, Mae Burrows, Helen Potrebenko, Penny G. (pseudonym), several inmates and ex-inmates (those who wished to remain anonymous), Bob Mercer, and Don Sorochan, QC.

To the publishing team at FriesenPress, I'm especially grateful to Publishing Consultants, Kim Schacht and Brianne Mackinnon for their consistently positive encouragement and prompt replies to my many questions and concerns. For the editorial and proofreading services of Wren Handman and Gisele Plourde respectively, I am most appreciative. For graphic design services, I am most grateful to the FriesenPress team. For her hauntingly beautiful front and back cover photography, credit goes to my very talented daughter/photographer, Erica Franz.

For legal services, I thank Don Sorochan, QC for his gracious generosity in providing me with a lengthy analysis of my text and for his invaluable advice and direction regarding the content. His critique was especially useful because, as a mediator during the forty-one hours of the hostage-taking, Don had first-hand knowledge of that tragic event and many of the people involved in it.

To several friends and family who, at a critical juncture in my writing journey, offered very useful editorial comment causing me to shift my focus ever so slightly but significantly, and in so doing, made my story much more engaging. For their wise counsel, I gratefully acknowledge Baiba Thomson, Michelle Morissette, Tom Little, and my husband, Tim Short.

For historical and cultural background on Riverview (Essondale) Hospital and Tranquille School, I thank Anna Tremere, former curator of the Riverview Hospital museum and past president of the once-active Riverview Hospital Historical Society. Her generous, constant, and unwavering support for my projects over the years, and her passionate intensity and knowledge of her subject material continue to amaze and delight me. Anna's magnificent lobby display on *BRAVE* night which featured three mannequins dressed in period costume, each representing a stage in Mary's professional life, was a show stopper.

For their extraordinary dedication and perseverance in locating the long-forgotten and buried *Proceedings in the 1976 Inquest on the Death of Maria Elizabeth Steinhauser*, I owe a huge debt of gratitude to Tej Sidhu, manager, Anita Tamber, program assistant and Laverne, program assistants, all of the B.C. Coroner Service, Metrotown, Burnaby. By unearthing this time capsule of word pictures, utterances, emotions, and glimpses into a time and place that no longer exists, this dedicated team helped me to make Mary's story come alive once again for a contemporary audience.

To my daughter Erica, I am very grateful for her considerable photographic talents in creating moving and powerful images for a series of Instagram photoessays of Mary's life, work, and legacy. See **In_Memory_of_Mary** or **mary_steinhauser.** The unique and memorable images in this IG record are simply amazing and serve as a promotional and educational vehicle carrying Mary's story to a global audience.

Finally, how deeply indebted I am to my husband, Tim, for his loving, unwavering support for my project. From the first day he learned that I would begin a long overdue rewrite and continuation of my story about Mary, he was with me one hundred percent. Always encouraging, always supportive, always understanding, and never once flagging in his confidence in me and in my ability to deliver a rich and carefully crafted story about a very brave young woman he never knew, but who just happened to be…my sister, Mary.

ABOUT THE AUTHOR

MARGARET (STEINHAUSER) FRANZ, THE YOUNGEST daughter of European immigrants to Canada, was born on Vancouver Island and raised in the West Kootenay area of south-central British Columbia, Canada. She graduated with a BA in Geography from Simon Fraser University, where she subsequently received her M.Ed degree.

An educator for most of her professional life, Margaret first taught at elementary schools in Toronto. After returning to B.C. and raising a family, she began lecturing at public and private post-secondary institutions in the Lower Mainland, finishing up her career on the faculty of the English Language Studies Department at Kwantlen Polytechnic University, Surrey B.C. At one point mid-career, she took a brief hiatus from teaching to work as an arts administrator, successful fund-raiser and avid promoter of the community arts in B.C.

Franz is currently retired, and lives with her husband and extended family in southwestern British Columbia. This is her first book.

CPSIA information can be obtained
at www.ICGtesting.com
Printed in the USA
BVHW091925100521
606472BV00003B/4